SECRETS OF THE BLUE JEANS MILLIONAIRE...

AND HOW YOU CAN USE THEM TO GET SUPER RICH!

T.J. ROHLEDER

(**a.k.a.** *America's Blue Jeans Millionaire*)

TABLE OF CONTENTS

Your Fortune is Waiting

by T.J. Rohleder

The above headline is amazing, but true!

It may sound like hype, but all the money you'll ever want and need is waiting for you!

Where is this money?

That's simple... It's in the wallets, purses, bank accounts, and available lines of credit that tens of millions of people are using on their credit cards right now.

These tens of millions of people are already spending this money like there's no tomorrow... They might as well be spending it with you!

Yes, there are tens of millions of people in America alone who are spending huge sums of their disposable income on a wide variety of products and services. All you have to do is get a very small percentage of them to spend their disposable income with you — instead of someone else — and you can make a fortune!

This book will show you how!

This book gives you 34 little-known marketing secrets that were first introduced on a very special 10-Hour Audio Program called 'Ruthless Marketing!' This Audio Program

---

contains the greatest marketing tips, tricks, and strategies we have used to make millions of dollars. Best of all, you can receive this powerful Audio Program — Absolutely Free! This is a $997 value — but it can be yours free! I'll show you how to get this Program free in a moment... But first, let me tell you a few things about myself...

Hi, this is T.J. Rohleder, a.k.a. America's "Blue Jeans Millionaire." I earned this nickname back in the early 1990's because, although I am a businessman who has brought in many millions of dollars, I am also the most average guy you'll ever meet, and I absolutely refuse to dress up for anyone.

Here's my story in a nutshell: For many years, I struggled financially and barely made enough money to keep a roof over my head. I was dirt poor and frustrated beyond belief! Why was I so frustrated? Because I hated to be poor and something inside of me knew there had to be a way to make a fortune.

I had heard about all kinds of average people who started with nothing and went on to making millions of dollars, and I believed that it was possible for me to do it!

But how did someone like me get rich? After all, I had no education, no special knowledge, skills and abilities, or any of the things you'd think it takes to make a lot of money. The one thing I did have, though, was the desire to get rich. So I began by answering business opportunity ads in the newspaper, and then quickly joined my first multi-level marketing opportunity in 1982. This led me to join even more MLM Companies over the next few years...

None of these MLM opportunities made me a dime, however, they did add a lot of fuel to my growing frustration about being poor. **In other words, they made me want to get rich even more!** Plus, these MLM Companies also taught me about goal setting and helped me realize that, if I was ever going to get rich, I had to improve myself and do even more.

Then, in 1984, I answered an ad in a supermarket tabloid and purchased a little booklet that was written by a man from Virginia, called...

"$25,000 For a Few Hours Doesn't Seem Fair!"

That little book taught me about two powerful wealth-making methods that captivated my imagination:

#1) Selling Information by Mail.

#2) Mail-Order Marketing (now commonly referred to as "Direct Response Marketing").

The author said that millions of people were looking for information on a wide variety of subjects. All I had to do was (a) find the hottest topics people wanted to know more about, (b) write a book, manual, or report of some kind that told people something interesting about this hot topic, and (c) sell the info-product through small mail-order ads in a national magazine just like the book he sold to me.

This one idea changed my life forever!

I became obsessed with publishing information and selling it through Direct Response Marketing ads and sales letters. It's all I ever thought about!

Then, shortly after I bought his book, I met my wife, Eileen, and that was the missing piece to my puzzle. Eileen was (and still is) very ambitious, just like me. She became excited about the idea of publishing and selling information by mail and wanted to do this with me!

So in September of 1988 — only 9 months after we were married — we published our first small booklet called "Dialing for Dollars." It was written to teach people about a very simple money-making idea that we

had stumbled onto for making money with an ordinary telephone answering machine. It was a simple plan, but one that we had actually made money with ourselves.

And to make a long story short, we ended up selling huge numbers of our Dialing for Dollars Program and brought in a total of...

Over $10-Million Dollars In Our First 5 Years!

Suddenly, we were rich! In fact, we had <u>more money</u> than we knew how to intelligently spend. But the most important thing was that we had discovered a powerful way to get rich by filling a growing demand that millions of people had for low-cost money-making plans and programs that actually worked and made money for the people who used them! We also discovered that the more we did to help our Customers make more money (by providing them with a variety of proven plans and programs), the more money we ended up making for ourselves.

How much money? Well, in our first 19 years alone, we generated a total of...

Over $114,000,000.00!

Yes, we started our little information publishing and Direct Response Marketing Company in the fall of 1988 with less than $300.00. And in our first 19 years, we brought in a total of over $114-Million Dollars!

So when I tell you that the huge fortune you seek is out there waiting for you <u>RIGHT</u> <u>NOW</u>...

I Know What I'm Talking About!

All you have to do is use our powerful marketing ideas to

offer people something they really want... Do this right, and millions of dollars can come pouring into your bank account!

Can it really be that simple?

Yes, it is! It's simple, but not always easy. In fact, the more money you want to make, the harder it can be. That's part of the challenge and should not discourage you.

And that brings me to the golden secret to your huge fortune!

Remember, all the money you want is waiting for you right now. I gave you part of the secret — which is creating informational products that people want the most. The other part of the secret to getting all of the wealth you seek is to...

Become a great marketer!

The more money you want to make, the more you must understand about marketing.

If you ask 1,000 different business experts what marketing is, you'll get some very complicated and confusing answers... But marketing is actually very simple. Here's my definition: Marketing is simply all of the things you do to get people to buy and re-buy from you as often as possible, for the largest amount of profit with each transaction. That's it! **When you learn how to do this the right way, you can bring in many millions of dollars — just like we have!**

Does that sound hard to believe? Well, it's true!

You see, the formula for wealth is so simple a junior high school student can understand it:

All you have to do is get enough people to continue giving you a large enough sum of money, for enough

profit from each transaction, and you will ultimately make many millions of dollars!

Hang that quote on your refrigerator or bathroom mirror!

Then think about this:

The better you become at marketing, the more money you will make!

And that's good news for you because this is exactly what you'll discover in this book!

Remember, this book contains some of the main secrets we shared on our 10-Hour Ruthless Marketing Audio Program that I recorded with five other marketing experts. *(In alphabetical order, the five experts who joined me on this program are: Don Bice, Ted Ciuba, Jeff Gardner, Chris Lakey, and Russ von Hoelscher.)* Together, all six of us shared some of our best marketing tips, tricks, and strategies for turning small sums of money into huge fortunes!

The bottom line: The fact that we learned how to become great in all phases of marketing is the secret that we used to turn $300.00 into $114-Million Dollars in our first 19 years...

This is the secret that can make YOU a fortune, too!

And that's what this book is all about!

I wrote this book by listening to the 10-Hour Ruthless Marketing Audio Program a few times and then writing a small summary on some of the best marketing secrets we discussed.

And now for the first time ever, because you are reading this book, you can receive my complete 10-Hour 'Ruthless

Marketing' Program — Absolutely Free!

Here's my special offer to you:

Recently, we held a special 2-Day Marketing Workshop here at our headquarters, called 'RUTHLESS MARKETING ATTACK!' **During this event, we shared our most aggressive and effective marketing secrets for turning small sums of money into a huge fortune!** We brought in a professional recording Company to capture the entire 2-Day Workshop and now the entire Program can be yours on easy-to-play Audio CDs and a GIANT Workbook that is jam-packed with 879 of our most aggressive marketing secrets. In addition, the entire package will come to you with other powerful bonus gifts worth many thousands of dollars, including the original 10-hour Ruthless Marketing audio program that will be yours free!

My offer to you is simple:

When you purchase our brand new 'RUTHLESS MARKETING ATTACK!' 2-Day Recorded Workshop, I will also give you the original 10-Hour 'Ruthless Marketing' Program that this book was based on — Absolutely Free!

This is a $997.00 value — yours absolutely free!

Here's how to get our original 10-Hour 'Ruthless Marketing' Program Free:

Find a computer. Get online. And visit...

www.FreeRuthlessMarketingProgram.com

Just visit our website right away. You'll read all about

this powerful new 'RUTHLESS MARKETING ATTACK!' Recorded Workshop and be shocked and amazed! As you'll see, this is the ultimate Program for using our most aggressive marketing methods to turn small sums of money into a huge fortune! You'll get all the details super fast. Then you can order this powerful Program right from our Web-Site. It's fast, easy, and 100% secure! We'll RUSH this powerful new Program to you — including all the free bonus gifts that you'll read about on our website. **Then, on top of everything else you'll receive — we'll also RUSH you the original 'Ruthless Marketing' Program — a $997.00 value — Absolutely Free!**

So please go through this book and discover the marketing secrets that interest you the most. Then think about all the ways you can use these secrets to make huge sums of money! Remember, the more you know about marketing, the more money you will make!

Your fortune really is out there waiting for you right now! The secret to getting this fortune can be found in the 34 secrets in this book and in the 10-hour Ruthless Marketing Audio Program that you can receive absolutely free!

So go through this book and discover some of our best marketing secrets that are in the original Ruthless Marketing Audio Program. Then go to www.FreeRuthlessMarketingProgram.com to find out how simple and easy it is to get your free 10-hour audio program that normally sells for $997.00! I hope to meet you in person in the near future at one of our marketing seminars and hear about your success story!

CHAPTER ONE

The best way to get someone to give you $3,000 is to get them to give you $300 first.

This marketing secret is oriented toward the fact that it's very difficult to ask a new customer for $3,000 — or in some cases, even $300 — right off the bat. The way to build your relationship and trust with them is to sell them a low-cost offer on the front-end, with your very first sale. You do that by selling something for $30, or $40, or $50.

As long as it's a low-entry price, this will work well — especially if you under-promise and you over-deliver. The reason you do that is because you don't really care about the profits on the front-end. **You're not going to get rich with your front-end sales profits, and anyone who believes otherwise is doomed to failure.** Ultimately, the purpose of that front-end sale is to build a strong relationship that will lead to lots more sales. Your customers really have to take a leap, that first time, even when there's a very low-end product involved. When they get that product and it's more than what they expected — and they believe it's worth ten times what they paid for it — you've started that relationship in the strongest possible way, you've locked it in, and now they're ready to go with you to the next step and purchase that $300 product, or that $3,000 product.

Here's an example of this principal in action. If you

watch infomercials (and as a student of marketing, you definitely should), you'll see that almost all the products advertised are very low-end items. For example, there's one marketer I know who sells a product on TV for about $40. When I asked him about how much money he was making selling that product, he said, "I don't make any money on it. In fact, I lose millions of dollars every single month selling that product. The infomercial alone costs hundreds of thousands of dollars to create." But, he said, "I don't sell that product to make money. I sell that product to get the people in, to qualify them, to build that relationship, and then I have my people on the telephone sell them a $2,000 product, then a $4,000 product, and then a $7,000 product! That way, **I don't have a problem losing millions of dollars on the front-end because I'm building up my customer base, I'm building those relationships, and I'm making $10 million to $30 million on the back-end."**

That idea of getting the people in, building the relationship with a low-cost front-end product, and then making your big profits on the back-end with higher-end products is a perfect strategy. "First you must win their trust, and then you win their money." The infomercial example is a powerful way of illustrating that. You may not know this, but **many marketers lose money on the front-end. All of their profits are made on the back-end.** A lot of marketers don't understand this at the beginning. One of my friends is a good example. When he was starting out, he once saw a full-page ad in a magazine that sold a $10 book. He said to himself, "I can write better copy than that! I'll put out my own ad." What he didn't know was that money wasn't being made at the front-end with that $10 book.

But that's how you have to start out in building that buyer-seller relationship. Look at it in terms of a romantic situation. When you invite someone to dinner, what you're really doing is hoping to form a relationship, so you might eventually invite them to your apartment. You can't say, right away, "Why don't you come to my apartment?" You might get a few takers, but not many!

Never forget that Direct-Response Marketing is supposed to be a personal medium.

You may be writing to ten thousand people, or even a million, but you've got to do it on a one-to-one basis. This is easy to do in Direct-Mail because the number one reason Direct-Mail is so popular, even in this Internet age, is that it's a medium based on one-to-one communication. **You're addressing your customer directly, appealing precisely to their needs.**

But that's not all. Never forget that you can also get personal with print advertising and on the Internet, especially if you target a niche market, and if the people who get your communication believe you are offering them something they really want and need. In other words, it's a personal message: you understand their hopes, their fears, their desires, and then you can be communicating personally. You must "get inside the gray mush." By that I mean the mind of the person who you're aiming your communication toward.

Always remember that a customer is wrapped up in his or her own self-interest. This is a basic part of being human, so you can't blame them. **Your customers want to know the answer to WIIFM: What's In It For Me? They don't give a**

damn about your company or how much money you want to make. They want to know how much money *they* can make, how much younger *they* can look, how much money *they* can save, or a thousand and one other reasons why *they* should do business with you. So if you're going to get their hard-earned money, you must come to them <u>with a personal message</u> that touches their heart. **Much more money is made by going after the emotions of an individual than by going after their intellect.** Get personal whenever you can!

When my mentor Russ Von Hoelscher started in this business more than 30 years ago and didn't have many customers, he used to write little personal messages to his customers along with his sales letters. Sure, it took time to write a little memo to them: *"Dear Jack, I want you to know this program really works. If you give it a try, you risk nothing with our money-back guarantee. Sincerely yours, Russ von Hoelscher."* But you know what? This worked like magic!

Of course, when you're sending out 50,000 sales letters you can't do that. But when you're first starting in this business, you can — and you should. Even if you're sending out 50,000 letters, get personal with people. **This is such an impersonal world that people are absolutely hit over the head by personal messages, and they'll respond to messages from people who they believe really understand them, who know what's inside them, and who know what their deep desires are.** To get rich, get personal!

Empathy is one of the most important aspects of any marketing campaign. You must show people that you care about them and that you feel their pain, so they can identify with you. At that point, you have the foundation for the sale. Plus, <u>they want to always feel that they're doing business with people who are just like them</u>, people who think like them and have the same views, outlooks, and convictions as they do. Don't be afraid to get very personal and talk about exactly what your product or service will do for them, and what it's done for you. Tell people, *"Even though we haven't met, chances are we're very much alike."*

This may all sound easy, but in reality, it's harder than it sounds. When writing copy, **it's easy to fall into the trap of talking to your customers as a *group*, rather than individuals.** This happens to us all sometimes. You have to watch your pronouns, or you'll be writing a sales letter and find that you're using terms like "people like you" or "people in your position," which is *not* what you want to do. When you do that, you've lost your focus. You have to go back through your sales letters and focus on the fact that you're talking to one person, and you need to use the proper pronouns to indicate that.

My friend Jeff Gardner has told me about one technique that's helped him quite a bit, and one that you can use if you're getting into copywriting. In any market where he's promoting a product, **Jeff tries to get a visual idea of *one* person in that market who represents that whole market.** He may even give them a name: Frank, Mary, or something like that. He visualizes their wants, their desires, and even what they look like, where they live, and what type of car they drive. Then, as he sits down to write the sales letter, he'll actually address it to them: "Dear Frank..." And then he tries to sell to just Frank or Mary, not the whole market for that particular product. Of course, after he's done he'll take out "Dear Frank" or "Dear Mary" and put in "Dear Friend" to make it more general. But by writing it to that one person it makes it a lot easier to focus on selling one-to-one, versus falling into the trap of trying to sell to the whole market. **If you do that, then you've distinguished yourself from the vast majority of people who haven't gotten that precision, and who aren't being personal.** By using that one little mental idea that you were able to hold onto, you've given yourself a tremendous advantage.

CHAPTER THREE

Selling is finding out what people want, and then letting them have it.

When people start thinking about what they want to sell, or they realize they want to get in business and make money, they tend to start by coming up with an idea for a product or a service — and then they try to find a market of people who want that product or service. But <u>starting with a product or service is the wrong way to go about it: in fact, it's exactly backwards</u>. **You have to start by finding a market, and then flip it around and find a service that that market wants.** Even then, even if you think you've found a market or you *know* there's a market out there for your product or service, that market may be too small. You may not be able to make any long-term profits off that market. Since long-term profits are your goal, the way to achieve them is to find a large, starving market with a large amount of discretionary income. The bigger the market, the more money you can make with that product or service. Let's put it more plainly: **to do well in marketing, no matter the product, you have to find out <u>exactly</u> what people (or more specifically, a group of people) really want, and then let them have it.**

The opportunity market is a perfect example. There are millions of people who want to stay home and make more money. Same with the diet market: millions want to lose weight. In the sweepstakes market, there are millions who want to win prizes and money. I could go on and on, but I think you get the point — your best bet is to <u>start with a group of people with a common bond or interest</u>, and work your product backwards from there to cater to that market. That's not being cynical, that's reality.

Because I'm in the opportunity market and it's something I'm familiar with and study a lot, that's what I'm going to focus on here. Like I said earlier, there are millions of people who want to make money from home. They're not lazy: they just want to work for themselves. They've tried working for "the man," and know there's no future in it. That market wants useful, proven information products they can use to prosper and earn a living. When you start by focusing on that market, you can find something in particular they're looking for and develop products and services to match what they want.

Speaking of wanting, I want to make one brief distinction between what people want and what people need. Usually they're different: sometimes the two can go hand-in-hand, but often they don't. **So don't focus on developing products and services that the market *needs* — instead, spend your time developing products that the market *wants*, and more likely than not you'll have a lot easier time making money.** That's where the real money is. <u>People often spend twice as much money on something they *want* than on something they *need*</u>.

A "want" is an unfulfilled desire. <u>That unfulfilled desire creates the vacuum for the product or service you want to sell</u>. It helps to visualize the situation, as my friend and colleague Jeff Gardner likes to point out. Let's say you have a group of people out in the middle of the Sahara Desert, and they've been out there for days and days. They're all sweating to death, and they don't have any water. Ultimately, they all know they're going to die — and the only thing they really have in their pockets is cash. Say you come along with one canteen of water. How many people are going to pony-up money because they want that water? You may say, "Okay, they *need* that water," and if you're any kind of human being you'll give it to them for free.

That was kind of an extreme example — very few wants are life-or-death needs. But here's how you have to look at it: **there are markets of people who are just as thirsty for products they want as for those people in the Sahara Desert would be for a glass of water.** If you go out there and you find the markets with that kind of a drive and a passion for something that they want — something they crave and have an unfulfilled desire for — you don't have to worry about coming up with product ideas because the market will tell you what they want, and what they're willing to pay for it. It's a very simple system, but it is making many people super rich! It's not about going out and trying to find products and develop products, but finding that key want or need, and then to find a way to fill it.

A friend of mine says something that's a little controversial, but it illustrates his point well: **he says he wants to sell donuts to fat people. He wants to sell heroin to drug addicts. He wants to sell porno to sex fiends.** Sure, these examples are metaphorical, he's not going to do anything illegal or immoral to make money by preying on people's addictions, and he's not suggesting that you do so, but you should look for markets with that kind of hunger. Find the people who are already hungry, who just can't wait to give you the money for what they want or need. He's also saying to make it simple on yourself. Go where the market is — don't try to create one where it isn't. Don't try to sell heroin to people as they're coming out of the church, go down to the seedy sides of town.

In short, my friend is saying that you should find the

market first, and then serve it. That's important because **too many people fall in love with a product or service,** and they want to try to sell it to everyone, the market be damned. But let me make this point again: *you must find the market first and then serve the market.* Some of the best Direct-Mail millionaires I know <u>based their products on existing products that they or someone else were *already* selling</u>. Let's say they find a certain book that sold 75,000 copies by Direct-Mail; they study that book and write a manual or book or CD that's is similar to that, and they sell their version. People are insatiable! If a person is a horseracing fan, they're going to buy more than one or two gambling books on horse racing. If they want to make money, they keep buying moneymaking products. To use the porno illustration: the person who has two or three porno magazines or videos is the best candidate to buy a hundred more. It's a very sound marketing principle that can make you huge, never-ending profits!

CHAPTER FOUR

"As long as it sounds good..."

One of the things we have to do as marketers is make things sound good. You have to make <u>big, bold, dramatic promises</u> to the prospective buyer. One of the things that Dan Kennedy taught me that I think relates very closely to this is the principle of selling people what they want, but then giving them what they *need*.

Let's look more closely at the principle of selling people what they want. Earlier, I discussed how, in the opportunity market, people want to make money. What they really want to do is to make money *without having to do a damned thing*. What people really want in the weight loss market is not just to lose weight, but to lose weight *without doing a damned thing*. That's why they flock to magic pills and other quick cures. **People want things that are simple, easy, fast, quick; they're looking for instant solutions.** Hey, I didn't create it that way! It's not my fault that this is what people want. And it's what they want.

Whatever you sell, you must make it *sound* good. Certainly, you have to be legal, and certainly you want to keep your customers satisfied because the first sale sets up the second sale. But **you have to make your product sound like the greatest thing since sliced bread, without going over the top** — and sometimes, it's really difficult to know if your claims are over the top. Sometimes you think something's really over the top, but the market doesn't perceive it that way. So how do you really know if you're making it too unbelievable?

There's a fine line between making your product sound good, and making it sound too good to be true. Don't go over the top, but you really do have to make it sound good, so it's very desirable and appeals to people's emotions. **It also has to appeal to the laziness that most prospects have;** this sounds cynical, sure, but the fact is that you're asking people to do a lot. Not only are you asking them to give up their hard-earned money, but you're also asking them to make a phone call or send a fax. You're asking them to respond to your ad in particular, when there are another dozen ads right there in front of their face that are *also* asking them to send their money. You have a lot of competition out there for the customers' money, and so it really is important to do what this principle suggests and really make it sound good.

One way to make it sound good is to make it sound simple. You can get bogged down in the details if you're not careful, **but an offer that's highly attractive and sounds good is invariably something that sounds simple. You take this pill and sleep, and you lose weight. Or you buy this product and it accomplishes "x" without you having to do anything.** Like I said before, most people want the benefit with the least expenditure of effort. So if you make it sound simple to accomplish, it always sounds good. Some of the most powerful offers are the simplest offers.

A marketer I know once told me, *"If you can't explain your offer and make it sound as great as possible in one minute or less, you need to go back to the drawing board."* Look at any of the great, successful offers out there — like those TV infomercials where they're selling real estate programs. If you closely look at it, sure, there are a lot of details. But the basic offer is simple: you can get rich buying and selling real estate, and we'll show you how. As long as it sounds good, **that can lead you into making an irresistible offer, where**

you just keep piling stuff on. Remember those old Ginsu commercials? "You get this great knife and also you get this paring knife and you get this scaling knife and, hey, we're also going to give you this free car!" They just throw everything in so at the end you go, **"Oh, my goodness! They only want $19.95? That's incredible! It's irresistible! That sounds so good I've got to get in on it!"** This is called **"the pile-on technique."** You stack up so much stuff, that in comparison to the amount of money you're asking for, the money seems inconsequential.

There are other techniques that will help your product sound good. Easy-to-read bullets that outline the advantages of your product are very effective. So are bonuses. **My friends and I sometimes buy information products — newsletters, for example — just because they offer five, or seven, or ten free bonuses.** Those free bonuses might be four-page reports that cost you a dime apiece to produce, but if the subject matter rings a bell in a potential customer's head, it might get them to subscribe to a newsletter that they would ordinarily have ignored. But you have to be careful with those bonuses! Marketer Ted Nicholas used to have a warning about freebies that I thought was especially cogent, since so many people will take things that didn't sell and add them as bonuses. He used to say, "That's always a mistake. **You want your bonuses to be so attractive and sound so valuable that people are willing to buy the product just because they want the bonuses."** So never, never add a bonus just so you can throw in things that didn't sell. That's shooting yourself in the foot, plain and simple.

CHAPTER FIVE

Write down your best ideas when they're new, when you're first getting started and are very excited, because these ideas are hot — and you'll need them later when you're cold.

Ideas are like slippery fish. They're hard to hold onto, so you have to capture them and write them down. I know how true this really is because for much of my life, I've made my living by selling ideas. First, you have to know that ideas aren't flashes of inspiration that some folks have and some don't. **Ideas are inspiration that comes from perspiration. That's why most people never have a good idea a year: they don't work at it.** I can't tell you how many times people have said to me, *"You have so many creative ideas. I just don't think that way."* Well, they're partly right. They have the right tools and they're just as creative, but *they don't use them.* They operate under the mistaken assumption that ideas just come to you, which isn't true; <u>ideas don't come except as a result of effort. You need to *work* for them</u>! It may not appear that way sometimes, especially when you see someone come up with an idea instantly, right before your eyes. But I can absolutely assure you that that idea bloomed because of the work and studying they had previously done, or because of the time they'd previously spent thinking about a similar issue. It's more of a style of thinking than anything else.

If you say, "I never have any good ideas," then I can guarantee you that it's because you haven't tried hard enough. You've never just put yourself down at a desk or table and done the background reading on the appropriate subject, and then spent time trying to come up with ideas until you found one that worked. **For every great idea that works, there are dozens of bad ideas that have to be rejected.** We tend to forget about all the bad ideas; that's reality. That's a part of the whole process. In any idea session, you want to <u>come up with as many potential ideas as possible, because most are going to be bad</u>. But you know what? It gets better with practice. The fewer times you sit down and do this, the more bad ideas you're going to have. In other words, **with practice, you're going to get a higher percentage of good ideas.** Your cerebral batting average will go up.

Frankly, <u>ideas are like photography.</u> Amateurs take a couple of pictures — maybe a roll — and then they compare their work to that of a professional photographer in a magazine. I don't know about your photos, but mine often have the red eyes, and they just don't compare favorably at all. In college, my friend Don Bice had an occasion to be on a project that was photographed by LIFE magazine. The photographer shot hour after hour, while his assistant changed the film. They went through more than 100 rolls of film that day. **They shot from every angle, bracketed every exposure, and they took a ton of pictures! They wanted to get the best picture possible. Out of all of those they took, the magazine ran one photograph, but it was an excellent one.** That's all you need when taking photos — the one that's a winner! It's the same thing with ideas. You go through a ton of them so you can find the one that's a winner.

Some people like to look at it as panning for gold — you end up with a lot of pebbles, and only a few are nuggets you can use. This is the point you should focus on: **you have to sift and sort through a lot of dirt and rocks and clutter and gravel before you find those gold nuggets.** I believe the one reason that people never find those gold nugget ideas is because they try to sit down and set their minds on finding that one, single million-dollar idea. They don't accumulate hundreds of ideas and then sift and sort to find that million-dollar idea. Heck, maybe it's not even there — maybe there are five or ten $100,000 ideas. You've got to be able to recognize them and keep them.

You shouldn't always be trying to get the home run all the time — in other words, don't go after that million-dollar idea to the detriment of all other ideas that might occur to you. Focus on just getting hits and getting on base — because **no matter how many ideas you have, you can never tell which ones are going to be home runs and grand slams! You can only discover that as you introduce them into the marketplace.** As the market embraces the ideas, they're the ones to tell you whether your idea's going to be a grounder or a home run or whatever. You just focus on getting good solid hits — you don't always try to hit over the fence all the time. It's a numbers game. The more ideas you have, the more potential gold nuggets you have. You go for quantity, as many ideas as you can — good and bad.

Inspiration can strike anywhere, not just in a brainstorming session. I don't know many good marketers who don't always carry a notepad everywhere they go, so they can write ideas down. You can come up with ideas at 3 o'clock in the morning when you wake up to go to the bathroom, or when you're in line at Starbuck's, or when you're driving down the highway. When you do, **you write it down. Keep a log, and go back and evaluate what you've written later.** That's where the breakthroughs come: when you're looking at the material you've already written and then you go, "Oh, yes, *that's* an idea I can use!" Sometimes you'll be able to fit two or more ideas together into a profitable whole. Or you'll be working on something totally different, and you'll remember something or refer back to your notes, and you'll see another idea you can tie in. That's why it's important to write every idea down – even if, at first glance, you might think it's not such a great idea.

My friend and colleague Don Bice has a friend who creates illusions for magicians; he's the one who came up with the vanishing Statue of Liberty trick for David Copperfield. He puts his ideas down in composition books. He just comes up with an idea for a trick, and he enters it on a page in a composition book. Then he'll think of another one and put it on another page. Sometimes he has no idea in the world how to accomplish the trick, but then later he comes back and he says, "I've got an idea about this one," and he'll jot a few thoughts down. He does that on occasion, and the first thing you know, a need arises and he says, "Oh, I know where there's a great idea," and he goes into his composition books and goes through them. He finishes it and completes it or changes it at that point. He doesn't have to sit down and start from scratch every time.

Ideas don't just come at you from nowhere. There aren't little inspiration particles flying through the universe that just happen to collide with your brain occasionally and cause new ideas. You have to work at getting them. Don't wait for them to come to you; make them happen. My mentor Russ von Hoelscher gets up in the morning, gets a pot of coffee going, then sits down with a yellow pad and forces himself to think. He writes down everything that comes to mind, regardless of how frivolous it might seem. *This* is how great ideas appear out of nowhere — by making those ideas happen, by giving them the time and the space for them to come to you.

And here's an integral part of that creative concept: **if you want better ideas, ask better questions.** I think, sometimes, you even have to ask yourself crazy questions. Ask yourself wild and outrageous things – impossible things! If you've got a company that's never done more than a half-million in one month, all of a sudden start asking yourself wild and crazy questions like: What would it take to get a million dollars a month? Other people would say, "Hey, that's impossible! You've never even done a half a million in one month. You've never broken that record, so what are you doing asking yourself what it would take to make a million a month?" Sometimes, **just by asking yourself hard questions about what it's really going to take to do what you want to do, all of a sudden you do come up with breakthroughs.** It opens up your horizon.

CHAPTER SIX

Follow the leader.

Clients are always calling me up and asking how they can find markets that haven't yet been tapped. They wonder how they can find those hidden markets that have the potential to be gold mines, the ones nobody's gotten to before. But I tell them, "Look, **you don't want to be a pioneer!** Pioneers get arrows in their backs. You want to be someone who follows the leader!" How do you do that? **Here are the four steps:**

1) When you find a hungry market, read the publications that target that market and determine the most successful companies currently promoting products there.

2) Find out what they're doing. How? Simply buy their products and get on their mailing lists. Instead of getting into the process of that company, many marketers will just look at the ads and think they can figure it out that way. But it's much more effective to step into that company — and you do that by purchasing their products. Spend some money on research, and get into the funnel to find out what comes next and next.

3) You need to ask yourself: "How can I model my business after them?" If they're already successful, you don't want to go off the track and do something different. **You want to model their success — but don't mimic them too closely.** Imitation may be the sincerest form of flattery, but it's also trademark infringement. Still, if you want fast success, the best thing you can do is model successful people and successful companies. This comes back to the second point, which is finding out what they're doing. One of my friends tells a story about seeing what he believed was a successful full-page ad that ran month after month in the money-making and opportunity magazines. It was placed there by a gentleman by the name of Mark Harrelson, who was actually losing money on that ad — but my friend didn't know that! What he found out later was that Mark was taking the names of all the people who were purchasing his product on the front-end, and he was making all of his money on the rental of those names. Because he didn't know the exact model and how Mark was making his money, he tried to model part of his own system on Mark's — but he failed completely because he didn't understand the system. You have to understand it all and model it as closely as possible.

4) Match them closely at first, but then figure out subtle differences you can exploit. You need to ask yourself: "How can I make my product better? How can I make people want it more than the competition's product?" Come up with as many ideas as possible. You may want to offer a stronger guarantee, more bonuses, better pricing, maybe installment payments, or more customer service, better help or advice, or whatever. You must do all you can to differentiate yourself from the company you're modeling yourself after. You want to make that successful company's model even better.

This four-step system is perfect because **what you're doing is taking something that's already been proven successful, and modeling your own system after it. You get the success fast, but now you're making it even better, so you're making even more money than the person who pioneered in that market.**

But most marketers want to come up with something completely new. Why don't they follow the leaders? Partly because they're afraid of competition. When most people are starting anything, they're surrounded by all kinds of fear and uncertainty. They say, "I need to get into something where nobody else is — where it's kind of a marketing wasteland." Well, you know what? It's a wasteland for a reason. You don't want to be in that kind of market; **you want to be in a market where you *know* that people are already buying, where hungry people are already giving their money to somebody else.** To put it a little crudely, you want to just belly up to the trough and start eating.

There's another advantage to being involved in a market that already has some big shakers and movers: they stir up the desire. This is especially true with the Internet. Now, the big guys in a market can't always close a sale, for a number of reasons. It could be the price, it could be the way it was presented. Or maybe, at the time the people interested in the product were too busy to deal with that particular marketer, or didn't have the money. But later on they come looking again — and guess who's sitting there waiting to help them? Statistically, **80% of the people who make an inquiry about a product eventually buy, but they buy from a company *other* than the one they made the inquiry to.** So if you're working in an isolated field, you're having to work harder — because you're not getting all those extra sales that other people have helped grease the chute for.

In many markets, a particular company can never meet the demands of all the potential customers. It's not just that their product range isn't broad enough. **In many cases, there's more demand for their products than a company can meet, because they can only create so many products and do so many mailings a year. If you get into an existing market, then, there's that leftover demand that the other companies can't profit from.**

Even if the pickings seem limited, sometimes you can

just walk into and meet that demand. In any market where there are multiple companies, you'll find that a particular client — let's call him Joe Schmoe — isn't just a client or customer of Company A. He's buying products from Company A, B, C, and D. If Company E jumps in there, he's going to be a client of theirs, too.

Here's another way to follow the leader. **I know of two instances where people have made fortunes just by learning information from people who were making a little bit of money.** David Bendah made millions of dollars with a book on how there are billions of dollars of unclaimed money. He got the information from a guy in Wisconsin who was writing little tiny ads. He talked to him and the guy told him, "I'm doing "x" amount of dollars ($500 a week or so)." Dave asked him, "Why don't you do more?" And he said it was enough. He was a schoolteacher, and was just happy to make this much. Bendah took the idea and made it into a bestseller. He didn't copy the guy's book, he rewrote it, made it completely different, and made over $1 million with it.

Then there's Les Brown (not the famous motivational speaker). He talked to a guy in Phoenix who wrote a book on the Hot Tracer Program. The guy told him everything he wanted to know about the program, and he built it into a $250,000 a year business. It was some of the sweetest money he ever made, because he worked about five hours a week!

So just tapping into who's doing what, and then seeing if they'll talk, can make you tons of money. It's amazing how many people will tell you exactly what they're doing. Once they do, you can do the same thing — only better.

CHAPTER SEVEN

Buckets of money on the back-end.

You can't get rich with one-shot offers unless you're selling something that costs many thousands of dollars. Therefore, most of your profits will come from the back-end. This is a message you'll have to learn and relearn in this business: in most cases, 99% of our profits will come from the back-end. If you're selling something on the front-end, you <u>want to get that "wow" factor</u>. You want the people to get it — whatever they paid for it, whether it's $10, $100, or $1,000 — and say "Wow! I can't believe I got so much value for my money! I got many times more value than I ever thought I would from this offer!" <u>You want them to be so impressed that they're ready to buy your back-end offer</u>, which can be much more expensive.

Of course, even your back-end needs a back-end. *Back-end selling never stops.* Constantly stay in touch with these customers because that's how you get rich in this business — by having back-end offer after back-end offer. **You should mail to them at least 10 or 12 times a year with new offers — and they should all be related.** Don't try to sell them a book on gambling, and then come back with a book on making money in mail order. You should always focus on the same product line.

It's also important to know **the lifetime value of your customer**. If you know a customer usually stays with you for

3½ years and spends, for example, $5,400 over that period, you know a customer's value, on average, is $5,400 over 3½ years. What you want to do then is some simple math about **how much you can afford to spend to get that customer.** I've already mentioned about how many marketers are willing to lose money, even substantial sums of money, to get a customer. **If you know a customer is worth $5,400 over time, you can probably double, triple, or quadruple the money you'd normally spend on the front-end just to get that customer.** So know the math of Direct-Response Marketing, and know that the buckets of money are always made by reselling to the customer over and over again.

Here's another principle that I happen to think is great: testing your new ideas and your promotions with your best customers first. If it won't work to your best customers, it's not going to work to anybody else. Let's take my pal Russ von Hoelscher as an example. His best customers are his 7,000+ newsletter customers. He makes offers to them, and within weeks he can tell whether he can send those offers out to the 20,000 or 30,000 other people on his customer list. If your best customers won't buy, your other customers *definitely* won't buy.

CHAPTER EIGHT

Keep baiting the mousetrap with the same cheese that snared them the last time.

Many marketers are guilty of ignoring this principle. We make a sale, and then we say, "What do I sell them next?" I've spent a lot of time asking myself this. Well, the secret is right there in front of us: **we should sell more of the same type of thing that they bought from you the last time.** People new to this business invariably come up with the solution that keeps them from earning more money. They keep looking for something different to sell to their customers, while the successful marketer looks for more of the same thing. That always just seems to come as a shock to newcomers. They say, "But I just sold them that."

Well, good! It's time to sell them the same thing again. Sometimes folks will buy the same thing again in a different form. If they bought the book, they'll buy the audio CD. If they bought the CD, they'll buy the video. If they bought the video, they'll buy the CD-ROM. Look at it this way. Suppose you had an ice cream store, and I came in yesterday and bought a cone of chocolate ice cream. I came back today. Are you more likely to sell me chocolate, or vanilla? Well, the answer is obviously I will probably buy chocolate again, because I probably have a taste for chocolate. That's why you make money selling people more of what they've been buying **because when you know what people have an appetite for, then you can**

pretty well predict what they'll want the next time.

Now, this doesn't necessarily mean you can sell them the exact same information, but often you really can. I can't tell you how many books, tapes, and manuals I've bought on direct marketing. I bet there's at least one subject where everyone reading this has bought about everything that they can afford. Most people have an appetite for certain types of information, with a craving for subtypes within that genre. **Once you've identified someone's craving, that's even better than knowing their appetite.**

When you get someone to buy once, you can be sure they have an appetite for something, **but chances are that when they become a multi-buyer — when they buy something from you more than once — you've identified a craving, and you can sell them over and over again.** That's why, when you're looking for new customers and you rent lists, <u>the list is important because it tells you what people have bought in the past</u>. You go looking for people with an appetite for what you're selling. If people have paid $295 or $300 for a product, you can bet your life they have a really strong appetite. **If they're multi-buyers, then you know they're absolutely craving products.**

Then you know exactly what to offer them: something as close as possible to what they bought before, but with an added a twist or gimmick to it. **Something that will promise them the benefit they want, but give it to them even easier and faster than what they bought before.** If they bought a book about getting started in Internet Marketing, then maybe you can add a product about how they can sell better, or put together auto-responder ads they can run instantly. If it was a 30-day weight-loss diet that they bought last time, maybe you can offer them a 10-day lose-weight-while-you-sleep diet. You see? You offer them the same thing they bought before, but a version that's faster, better or newer.

It's the same for future products. At some point, people may get tired of the same thing. They've taken the same bait over and over, and they want something new. When I went to the ice cream store, I bought chocolate. I bought chocolate again and again, until finally I got tired of it. Well, the guy at the store's not going to say, "Well, why don't you take vanilla?" He's going to offer me deluxe chocolate with peanut butter, or something similar — **something very close to what I need, even when I wanted something different.**

So, when your customers start to tire of the bait you're offering them, you can give them a couple of choices. You can sell him something slightly different, or you can sell him what he needs next to move him toward his primary goal, dream, benefit, or whatever he's looking for. If you sell a customer several manuals on making money on the Internet — well, when those stop selling, you can offer him what he needs next: a website. If you sell him a website, then what does he need? He needs traffic to that website. Now you can offer several ways of getting traffic: advertising, giveaways, contests, news release packages, and on and on. Did you change the bait? Somewhat. The dream is making money with the Internet. **You're just tweaking your offer to move the customer along by saying, "Here's what you need next."**

When the mice stop taking a bait of American cheese, you're not going to catch them by switching to worms. Try cheddar! *Cheese* is what they want, so all you do is change the variety. Your customer's no different. **You just need to identify the cheese, and be prepared to offer him as much variety as it takes to make the sale.**

Many years ago, my mentor Russ von Hoelscher did some critiques of sales letters from a guy in Brooklyn, New York, who was selling horse racing information. He got to talking about his customers, and said that over a 10-year period he'd put together about 45 or 50 different manuals on horse racing. *How to Speed Race Horses, Horses for Turf Courses, How to Bet Horses on What the Odds Are —Especially Prior to the Race,* and on and on. He said some of his best customers over the past 10 years had bought all the manuals that he'd produced. Russ said, "My gosh, that's incredible. You mean they just keep buying horse racing manuals with slightly different variations?" He said, "Yep. If I put out five new manuals this year, my best customers will buy all five." He was charging around $50 a manual, which back then was a pretty good price, but certainly not an exorbitant one. These people could not get enough of horse racing information.

That's the whole premise behind one of the more savvy marketing techniques that you see some of the more savvy marketers using. That is, they offer a newsletter or an Internet membership site to their customers. What goes with every transmission, of course, **is another opportunity for the customer to get happily involved with your products and services, and those are the best people you could ever sell to** — the ones who are already your fans, who trust you, and like your message. When you recommend something new, they're waiting to pounce on it.

You see, you don't just create a single product — **you create a line of products.** In this business, we always talk about the back-end, the items that backup that first sale you make. **Remember, you need to have lots of back ends.** This creates a line of related products that move someone from beginner all the way up the spectrum. Too many people, in the beginning, forget about the line of products that they need, and they just focus on a one-time sale. People also forget that consumers are insatiable. That's the one message Alan R. Bechtold drives home so successfully when he tells his story of *Playboy* and *Penthouse.* The way Alan explains it, when the publishers of *Penthouse* saw that *Playboy* was making money hand over fist, they went into business with their own skin magazine. The critics at the time (the early

1960s) said, "Oh, there's no room in the marketplace for two magazines like *Playboy*. It just won't work!" Well, they were wrong, weren't they? I know this is an extreme example, not to mention a controversial one, simply because of the subject matter. But the truth is, the pornography industry makes a good model to illustrate the concept of insatiability. **People are never satisfied with just one product: they want more of the same.** So *Penthouse* made more by giving them less clothes! And now instead of two magazines, we've got maybe 200 of these skin magazines selling regularly and making all kinds of money. It just shows you that the people who buy that kind of product just keep buying, from all the different publishers.

Once upon a time, my wife said something about pornography: "Don't men realize that if you've seen one, you've seen them all?" But the truth is, of course not! Not all men buy pornography, but those who do are driven by their emotions, however unpractical or difficult that would be to describe. ***All* customers are driven by emotion. People always buy for emotional reasons.** And those reasons are the driving forces that make them want to continue buying MORE of whatever they bought the last time... Who's the most likely to buy a diet book? Someone who bought a diet book last month. Who's going to want that new porno magazine? They guys who are already buying that kind of magazine.

CHAPTER NINE

What people want is the magic pill.

What's the magic pill? **It's the one product or service that's going to make everything okay.** It's going to solve some major problem or offer your prospects a miracle cure. It's an instant and ongoing solution. I often use this metaphor of a magic pill because if people could pop a pill and have some great thing happen in their life, they'd buy it up like crazy.

For example, let's say you had a magic pill that, if someone swallowed it, would make them a million dollars overnight. Would they buy it? You'd better believe it. People would be lining up around the block for that kind of product. That's why you need to focus on creating that kind of an aura around your existing product. You need to look at it and ask yourself some really great specific questions: How can I take the existing product that I have and turn it into this magic pill? What can I offer? What can I add to that product? If I can't take the existing product and make it this magic pill type of an offer, what can I add to it to give it the aura of a magic pill deal?

Let me give you some examples of this. Remember how I talked about *wants* versus *needs* in another section? Let's look at weight loss. We all want to be healthier; we all want to be thinner. We all want to be in better shape. I can tell you in one second exactly what anyone in the world needs to do to lose weight: exercise and eat less. Boom! There you go.

I've basically just taken all the information from of all those weight loss books and boiled it down to just a phrase. *But people don't want that.* Eating right is difficult, and exercising is difficult and painful. People want that magic pill. That's why all these companies aren't telling their customers to eat right and exercise. What they're saying is, "Hey, I've actually got a magic pill! If you take it every night before you go to asleep, you're going to start losing pounds. They're going to just magically melt away!" It's a magical, miracle cure.

It's the same way with hair loss. They have these pills out now that will cause your hair to stop falling out — and you actually may grow some back. They really work, too. Of course, in the ads they don't tell you the pills are going to give you terrible halitosis and you're going to become impotent, because that doesn't sell very well. But they do tell you if you take this magic pill, that's all you have to do. You don't have to do anything else. If you can pop a pill, you can get the benefits. *That's* what people want. **People don't want a lot of hard work and effort.** They don't want to put years and years into something to get what they want. Whether it's weight loss, more money, more hair, or a new house, they want that magic pill that will give them <u>instant gratification</u>. The more closely you can turn your existing product into that magic pill, the more you're going to be able to make more money by hitting the wants of your prospects dead center.

If you've got an existing product, you should really focus on turning it into that magic pill — or at least try to do so. But so many marketers just don't understand this principle. Why? Largely because they don't believe that they *have* that magic pill — so they don't bother trying to give it that aura. But you have to try. **I believe you can take almost any product, with the right type of marketing and the right type of an offer, and get that type of magic.** It may not be the absolute magic pill with no drawbacks and no side effects, but you could certainly move it in that direction.

Let's take a closer look at the hair loss product I mentioned before. If you really looked at the product and its side effects, then you really probably wouldn't call it a magic pill. It doesn't work for everybody. It has these noticeable side effects, like I mentioned. One of the crazy things about this pill is that they're selling it based on sex appeal. If you lose your hair, will your wife or spouse or girlfriend still love you? Well, probably, but they don't want you to consider that. Heck, the truth is that if you pop this pill, even if your hair stops falling out and actually starts growing back, well, yeah, you're going to have your hair — but you're also going to have bad breath, and you're going to be impotent. Oops! The sex appeal doesn't work in that case. But you know what? It's painted as a magic pill because it can save your hair, and to guys who really want to keep their hair that's exactly what it is.

Why does the magic pill approach work? Think of it as the Microwave Society Syndrome. **We want everything fast.** We want it sure. We want it right away, whether it's weight loss or making money. If you told people, "Now, here's a great way to make money: you work very hard and don't spend too much, and at the end of five years you're going to have a big bank balance." A lot of people would say, "That's crazy! Here's someone who has a book on how I can make $10,000 a day while I'm lazy as a mud rat! Why should I listen to you?" **People are looking for instant cures for all their pain, and they're looking for instant gratification.** As marketers, what we have to do is sell the sizzle — but we have to deliver the steak. In other words, we have to sell all the things that really push the buttons on our prospects, but at the same time we have to give them some realistic items that they really will have to do if they're going to achieve the goal they want.

Let me tell you how we're doing this for our company. **We sell Direct-Response Marketing distributorships and dealerships.** We supply our customers with a product to sell and the sales material they can use to go sell it. Our most

---

successful distributors do a variety of things to achieve success, but of course we have a lot of other distributors who want someone else to do it all for them. **So what we're striving to do, more and more, is to create services within our company that offer to do almost everything for the customer.** We do web design. We do web hosting. We do all the typesetting on the postcards for them. We go out and find the best mailing lists. We print the postcards for them. Then we send them the postcards every single month along with the mailing lists, and all they have to do is lick and stick while they're watching television.

For some of our customers — not all of them — that's exactly what the magic pill is. We tell them, "Hey! You can do it in as little as five or ten minutes a day!" That's what they want: a way that they can be in the mail order business, when all they have to do is sit around licking and sticking. Actually, they don't even have to lick, because the mailing list comes on self-adhesive labels — and so do the stamps. Then they just go and drop them into a post office box, **everything else is done for them.** That way, in all of our ads we can keep that message in front of the prospects and customers: that we'll do almost everything for you. **We just keep driving that message into them over and over again, because that's their magic pill.**

Here's another example. Russ Von Hoelscher tells about a woman he knows who made $1 million last year. She first started out with a product where she told people that they could mail her program. She'd give them the sales material; she'd tell them where to get lists. It was pretty successful. But then she realized that thousands of her customers didn't even want to do that. Finally, she instituted a program where she not only produced all the sales material, the program itself, and everything else — she also shipped it for them. That's right: she actually did all the mailing for them. She told her clients, "You can send me anywhere from a

$200 to $2,000, depending on how many pieces of mail you want me to send out with your name on it." The response was overwhelming. The money came pouring in. Because she was a good woman and tried to do her best for her customers, some of them actually made money. But the point is, **she did everything! Boy, did they love it.**

So there's a principle to consider. **The more we can do for our customers to make it easy for them, the better.** This doesn't just mean selling them information, it could work with anything. Whatever you sell, the more complete it is, the more thorough it is, the more it answers all the questions and is a complete system regardless of what type of product or service it is, the more your customers will love it.

·

CHAPTER TEN

Develop the right offer, and you'll attract the person you're looking for.

The bait you throw out there determines the type of person you catch. Furthermore, **for every person there exists a bait that they *cannot* resist swallowing.** With this powerful principal, I have hit on one of the most important lessons you can learn as a marketer. I've nibbled at the edges of this principle in other sections, but this time **I want to focus on the bait itself: the requirements for developing the right offer, and therefore attracting the right person you're looking for.** This is important because your overall moneymaking strategy depends on you attracting the right kind of people.

Now, if you're attracting the wrong kind of people, you may make a little bit of money — but your overall marketing strategy will suffer. Do you want to attract a person who's dependent, or independent? Are you looking for someone who's rich, or someone who *wants* to be rich? The answers to those questions will influence the kind of offer you use to attract your customers. **It's very important that you know exactly who it is that you're trying to reach.** Your long-term marketing plan depends on you attracting the right kind of people, folks who are likely to purchase from you again and again. It's not just the front end marketing, that first thing that you sell, it's also remembering that you want to attract the kind of people who will do business with you for years to come.

In our business, we use **the fishnet analogy.** If your business services people who prefer fine fillets of some particular ocean fish, you obviously want to cast your nets where you'll catch the largest number of fish. It doesn't serve you any purpose at all to catch a bunch of other kinds of fish because that's not your market. You're not selling to people who need that kind of fish. In the business world, your offers are your fishnet. **You have to cast your fishnet** (or fishing lines as the case may be) **in the direction of the people you most want to do business with — the people who you want to be your customers for the long-term.**

For your market, **you just have to find out what that bait is that the consumer can't resist swallowing.** In the previous sections, I've discussed all kinds of unique selling positions, and things you can do to make people feel like they have to respond to your offer. That's the bait we're talking about. I can't tell you what it is for your product; you have to figure that out for yourself. Find out what that one bait is, that one thing that your customer can't resist swallowing, and give it to them. **Give it to them over and over again throughout your offer, and you'll find that more of your customers will respond to those offers.** That will build the kind of long-term customer you're really looking for.

A lot of people don't understand this principle at all. **Here's an example.** We had this guy working for us for about eight months. He saw our company mail millions of pieces of mail before he got fired. Now he's back to selling cars. I ran into him a few weeks ago, and he started telling me about all these Direct-Mail pieces he's been mailing out, pieces he'd spent a couple of thousand dollars on. I asked him, "What's your offer?" and he said, " I don't have any offer." I guess the idea is that because he saw us sending out millions of pieces of mail, if he did a bunch, he was going to make money too. I see this with other people all the time: they think it works like that movie *Field of Dreams* with Kevin Costner. "If you build it, they will come." That was the theme of that movie, but you know what? That was a movie. It was a fantasy. A lot of people have this crazy idea that just because they're obsessed with their product or service, just because they absolutely love it, they can introduce it to the world and all these people are just going to flock to them. That's a gross misunderstanding of the way the world really is.

You can have a product for sale, but that doesn't mean you have an offer to sell it; and if you don't, you're sunk. **There has to be a reason why people should respond right now, and that's all tied into your offer.** In the car salesman's case, just thinking you can send something out in the mail without an offer attached to it is stupid; it's a bad marketing strategy. But that's the way a lot of people think. They haven't figured out that you have to have some kind of offer, some reason why people should do business with you. The offer's all part of a master scheme involving your overall marketing strategy.

An offer, as I see it, is something specific to get people to take action: a special sale that's going to expire on a certain date, or a special price, or a limited arrangement that really is only available now. **You need to look at the offer as the total package.** The price point, the payment terms, the bonuses that come with it, the reason for acting now, the primary benefit that's exploited when they purchase the packaged offer; all that together creates the final offer.

CHAPTER ELEVEN

Spend more money to reach fewer, more highly qualified people.

Another key to marketing success is to find the highly qualified prospects who are the most likely to buy whatever you have to offer. **This is what niche marketing is all about — spending more money to reach fewer but better qualified prospects or customers.**

First of all, **you should consider segmenting your customer list.** If you haven't figured it out by now, **your customer list is the single most important asset in your business.** There are different ways of segmenting that customer list — by what the customers buy, the types of product that they buy, the frequency of their purchases, the dollar amount of their purchases, or how recent they made their purchases. Those are just the main ways that you can segment your list. The number one question always has to be, **"Who are my best customers?"** Once you figure that out, set the criteria on a certain amount of money that they have to spend to qualify to get on a *different* customer list.

Once you have these different customer lists, you can communicate to people a little bit differently, based on what they bought in the past or how much money they've spent or how long they've been with you. That's one really good way to segment your customers. If you have customers who have been doing business with you for years, you could talk to them differently because you know they're very familiar with you. **You have to build a bond with your customers:** that's key. You have to stay in touch constantly.

By segmenting your mailing list to find that smaller group of best customers, **you're now able to spend more money to reach that smaller group.** You're not as confined, now, to the mathematics. Normally there's the cost of printing and postage to consider, but it goes out the window when you have that smaller group of customers to deal with. You can spend a lot of money because you can afford to; **you know you'll get a lot more back if you prime the pump.**

This is something that I've known about for years, but it was my friend Jeff Gardner who **recently reminded me about its true power.** I saw one of Jeff's mailings. In that mailing, not only did he have a 22-page sales letter and an 8-page insert and all these other nice printed pieces, but he took a brand new crisp $1 bill and glued it to the letter. Then he packaged it all up into a really beautiful plastic envelope that's three or four times more expensive than most envelopes you'd use in a Direct-Mail campaign. To get something like this in the mail — and I know this because now we've copied Jeff's model with some of our own customers — costs about $3, especially when you count the labor costs, because you can't machine-insert this kind of package. They have to be done by hand. The dollar has to be glued on with a special expensive glue like the kind they use on Post-it notes. Your security measures have to be beefed up a little bit, to keep people from stealing from you. There are simply a lot of little things that have to be done.

So you're spending $3,000 per thousand mail pieces just to get the offer into the mail stream. But, the point is, if it's only going to your very, very best customers, who cares if it costs $3,000? Who cares if it costs $10,000 per thousand? Sell a few of your items, and you'll make all that money back. **The point is not how much it *costs* you but how much it *makes* you.** That's the only thing you should be concerned with. Now, in order to not spend too wildly, you should test a more expensive version against the less expensive version. But the point is you shouldn't be afraid to go out there and be very aggressive, and be willing to spend quite a bit of money in your communications and your different promotions to your better customers. **You'll spend more money to reach fewer but better qualified prospects.**

Keep in mind that **this works only if you have a niche market you know inside out: one where you're able to get a high response rate.** At the time Jeff was sending out his offer, he had a best-customer list of only 300 or so, but he was able to get literally a 25-33% response rate. That's one out of every 3-4 people on the list purchasing a product. I'm are not talking about a $5 or $10 product, where they don't have to think about it to make the order, I'm talking about a $1,000 product. It made sense to spend more money on this smaller market because Jeff knew them so well that he knew that he could get a very high response rate. Sometimes he'd spend $3, $4, $5, or more per mailing.

Jeff recently told me about a telephone conversation he had with a gentleman who was marketing to his own niche group. He was just building up his business. He said something that stuck in Jeff's mind, and he actually had to slap the guy on the wrist a little bit. The other marketer said, "I'm going to start out with small postcards because I want to do this very cheaply. I know it's a good niche market, but I'm always going to do it cheap, cheap, cheap." Jeff told him, "You shouldn't think that way because sometimes the best money you can spend is in putting out a slightly better package, putting in some grabbers, making it more attention-getting, making sure the envelope gets opened so you get that bigger response. If you're always thinking about your bottom line and not about what's going to get the best response and bring in the most sales, you're never going to reach your ultimate goals." So here's the gist of it: **you have to look at not just what your bottom line is on mailings, but what that marketing is going to bring you back.**

I think some of that goes back to the principle that perception equals reality. If you're trying to sell something that's high dollar and it's perceived as something that's elite and ultimate, you have to put some bells and whistles into the package that are congruent with your pitch — that is, the message you're trying to put across.

Here's another example of that. There have been a lot of ads over the years saying "Send me $1, and I'll show you how to get $1 million!" The funny thing about most of those ads is that they look like they've have been put together by vandals, certainly not by someone who knows anything about graphic design. It certainly doesn't say, "Here's a millionaire placing this ad." You're supposed to send money to this person who obviously doesn't *have* a million dollars. Maybe they don't even have two nickels to rub together, and they're supposedly going to show you how to make a million bucks. That just doesn't work. **You do have to have a congruent message.** If you're going to be doing cheap, cheap, cheap all the time trying to sell anything — especially moneymaking information — you'll never make much because there's not a congruency between what you're actually putting out there and what you're selling. It's worth spending extra money, then, on elaborate and expensive mailings to people who've already demonstrated that they're good customers. Don't pull out all the stops on folks who haven't demonstrated their value to you as a customer. That's all part of segmenting your customer list and knowing whom your better customers are. There's something called the 80/20 rule, and it says that **20 percent of your customers are going to represent 80 percent of your profits.** In some of businesses, it's more like

90/10: ten percent of your customers represent 90 percent of your profits, and it's up to you to try and determine which 10 percent or 20 percent are the best. **You have to have qualifiers on their value.**

One way is to qualify people by how much money they spend. You'll find that a person who'll spend $200 is a better customer for you than someone who'll spend $29. First you get a responder, then you try to turn that responder into a buyer, and *then* you try to turn that buyer into a customer. **It takes about three sales before you have a real customer.** That's the 10-20 percent of your list you need to aim for. Those are the folks you need make test mailings to because you know that if they respond, you'll get good response from the other 80-90 percent. Those are the customers who will tell you whether your offer is good or not.

CHAPTER TWELVE

"The Hand."

Every offer or promotion that you create must meet these five crucial criteria:

1. Is it the right offer?

2. ...to the right person?

3. ...through the right media?

4. ...with the right hook?

5. Does it fit together with some kind of long-term plan?

There are many different marketing methods, but only a handful of them are vital. **This simple formula lets you focus on the essentials.** I attribute this marketing formula to Bill Graham, one of the greatest rock-and-roll promoters who ever lived. Bill had five key areas that every concert had to fall under. He called it his 'hand' — so I created a marketing formula that did the same.

Let's get right back to the offer. Remember, **the offer is *not* the product. The offer is everything that surrounds it.** It's the bonuses. It's the importance of time because there's a limited quantity. It's given to you because you're a special person involved in this kind of thing. Is it the right offer? In other words, is the offer good?

Then there's the second "finger" of the hand. **Is it going**

to the right person? Obviously you have to get the right person. If a magazine comes into our house and it offers beautiful, expensive clothing, if it's up to me that thing's going to find its way into the trash can because I'm digging through looking for Direct-Mail packages I can add to my swipe file. However, if it comes in and my wife's looking at the mail — well, she's going to pull out the catalog and she's going to throw all of the other stuff in the trash!

You also have to get your offer there though the right media: in the above case, I was talking about Direct-Mail. People who've bought from Direct-Mail are your best prospects to approach by Direct-Mail. People who buy on the Internet are the best prospects to approach on the Internet.

Next, you need to have the right hook because every buyer is motivated by a number of different things. As I mentioned in a previous section, <u>everybody has some bait that they can't resist responding to</u>. Our job as marketers is to find what that bait is. Is it the fact that what you're offering is so easy that it practically does itself, or is it the fact that it's going to make you feel special? I'm talking about that $75,000 convertible Mercedes I mentioned earlier. What will your audience respond to? Part of this is in the packaging. If you're offering to tell people how to make more money, don't send them a crappy mailing that looks like it's been run off on a photocopier 100 times.

Then there's the fifth point. **Does it all fit together with some kind of long-term plan?** <u>Every action, every promotion, every marketing approach, every offer should be leading your buyers to the next market, to the next approach, the next sale</u>. Let's suppose you do landscaping, and you're building decks. People who respond to that deck promotion can be given things in the offer that also encourage them to be proud of the fact that they're keeping their neighborhood clean, are building it up, and are being good citizens —

---

because what do you want to do after you sell them a deck? You want to put up a fence for them, or you want to put in the Jacuzzi.

So again, you should work on these things as isolated events; **try to be as creative as you can, and act on every offer like it's the only offer and the last offer you can ever make.** At the same time, however, it needs to be fully integrated so that it's part of a whole deck — one of the 52 cards, even though we might be doing a trick with the joker or the ace. It's part of the whole deck, and it's taking you where you want to go.

So my concept of the "hand" for business goes one better on Bill Graham's. One thing many people don't realize about Graham was that he only had a handful of ideas. If one finger was missing, then he could walk away from a project; **all five principles had to be there for it to work.** Everybody thought he was such a genius, but the truth was that he just had five good, solid principles that he used with every single deal. That doesn't mean his process was a bad one, quite the contrary. I think it's great when you can reduce your process down to five points because it's easy to memorize. Once you commit it to memory, you can commit it to action.

Modeling other successful people is important. Sure, we're all looking for creativity and that's good, but we should also recognize a formula that's working well for others when we see it. We get their mailing piece, we go to their website, and we find out through trial and error and investigation that they're making a lot of money, so we want to do something that's very similar — not to copy them word-for-word and design everything the same as them, but to capitalize on their success. **You can make a fortune just by copying success.** That's what I was doing with Bill Graham: I took that story and found a way to integrate it into Direct-Response Marketing. Some of the richest people in our business do that

— they take ideas from other industries, just like that McDonald's exec took the concept of drive-in banking and adapted it for fast food. They adapt the idea to what they're doing, and the success comes.

That's what the great Broadway promoter, Billy Rose, used to do. He said, "Hell, anybody can write a Broadway show. All I do is look at the Broadway shows and find out what works. Every show needs an opening. Every show needs a dramatic piece, and every show needs an 'I'm down but I'm going to get back up' piece." He assembled shows by that formula, and it worked again and again.

Now, don't let the term "formula" put you off. Most people think using a formula takes away the creativity. The truth is that it's just the reverse. **A formula is a guideline for ideas.** It's a yardstick along the way to help you get along a proven path. So formulas are very useful, and they don't necessarily restrict creativity.

CHAPTER THIRTEEN

What you really sell.

You must *never* fall into the trap of selling products or services; **you sell *concepts*!** You sell ideas, benefits, end results, and solutions. **Believe it or not, products are secondary.**

I've got the perfect story to go along with this point, one provided by my friend and colleague Jeff Gardner. He was recently talking to a copywriter, who was telling him about some of the people he'd worked with and some of the projects he'd done. There was this one person who did a lot of Direct-Mail, and he came to the copywriter and said, "Look, I need you to write this hot eight-page letter about a new program we've put together, one that will help people beat the slot machines in any casino anywhere in the world. I'll pay you $2,000 to write it this letter." The copywriter said, "Hey, that's great! It sounds like a great offer. Go ahead and send me the book and I'll get started." The guy said, "Well, there's no book." The copywriter asked, "There's no book? How am I supposed to write the letter?" The guy said, ***"You just write a hot letter selling this program, and then I'll worry about coming up with the program itself."***

That's really the key to making money: **you have to have a great offer.** A lot of people fall in love with products. After they've developed a product and spent years and years honing it and polishing it lovingly, they decide that maybe it's time to sell it. They've thrown all this money into it, after all. But what if it doesn't sell?

The secret to avoiding this outcome is to do things the other way around. **First you come up the hot offer, the great idea, the great concept;** *then* **you decide what product can fit into that concept.** That's really the key to making money — not falling into this trap of starting with the product. Don't be product-centered, where all your focus is on the product; you need to be market-centered instead.

Hot products are a dime a dozen. I get people calling me all the time saying, "I've got a hot product, and everybody wants it." That really makes me cringe because it's rarely the case. How many perfect products are there that just magically sell themselves? How many products are there where a person can stand on the street corner and say, "Hey, I've this hot product," and people will rush up with a handful of cash and want to buy it? **People have wants and desires, sure, but those are magnified by great marketing — by creating these great concepts and ideas and benefits, and the end results and solutions that go with them.**

Let's say you decide to target the weight-loss market. All these people are heavier than they want to be; they all have a problem, but they don't have a particular product in mind to fix it. They're not saying, "I want to have something that works my abs. I need a plastic product in the color red that straps me to the ceiling so I can do a flying motion!" See what I mean? They don't have any product in mind, **they have a** *benefit* **in mind. They have a** *solution* **in mind.** They want to lose that weight in any way possible — especially if it's easy. **So what you do then is create the hottest offer, the hottest concept you can, that will satisfy their desires.** In this market, the hottest concept would be that magic pill I've already discussed. With this famous magic pill you don't do any working out, you don't even change how you eat. You continue to sit on the couch watching TV, eating bonbons, and Ben & Jerry's Ice Cream, but every night before you go to bed you pop that magic pill and the pounds melt away while you sleep. Once you have the concept of the magic pill, then it's time to go to the scientists and the research department people and say, "Okay, now we need to create this magic pill."

That's the secret to making money. **You focus on the marketing and the concepts and on filling those wants and desires, and then you work backwards.** You reverse-engineer and then come up with the product. Using that type of a system, you can become incredibly successful a lot faster than the other way around, where you focus on the product and then you tear your guts out trying to find a way to market and sell it.

In other words, people don't want products at all. **They just want the benefits and advantages the products give them.** For example, the front-end sales letter we're using right now was written 12 years ago. When we wrote it, we had absolutely no product to go with it whatsoever. But we knew our market and wrote the sales letter to match it, and we tailored a product to fit it. Since then, we've changed the basic product several times, and we still use the same letter. The advantages and benefits of what we offer are what count — not necessarily the product itself.

Now, I realize that some people just have a real problem with this. They think it's almost a scam to create the ad copy first, and *then* create the product. I think one of the challenges with it is that a lot of people have, somewhere in their mind, that one product, book, idea, or invention that they know will make millions. Let's say you go out and stop ten people on the street and ask them, "Do you have an idea right now for a new product or book that would make you rich?" You're probably going to get seven to eight people who'll say, "Oh yeah, I've this great idea for this or that." They're product-oriented. They would never think of identifying a need and then creating a product to fill it; they think the product is supreme.

Obviously that's the wrong way to think, but it's just the way people are. We all come up with these great things and inventions that we think would sell like hotcakes, but we don't really think about who we're going to sell them to. I believe that if they think about it, most people don't have a huge problem with the marketing coming first. Sure, some will say, "That's not really genuine because you're trying to manipulate them. You're trying to manipulate their desires." But the way I look at it is that **you're fulfilling desires that already exist. You're delivering exactly what they want.** I think the world would be a better place if, instead of us trying to push products onto people that they don't want, we went out and found out what people really wanted, and then worked our hardest to give them that. I really think that's the key to ultimate happiness.

CHAPTER FOURTEEN

The destination comes first, and then you pull out the map and begin planning the trip.

When you're on a marketing mission, you have to start by focusing on your end game — that is, the result you're looking for — and then build your road map to riches based on that destination. In our market, we often fantasize about making a million dollars. For many of us, that's a goal that's way out there; it's hard to think about making a million dollars a year. So, instead of worrying about making a million dollars a year, or whatever your endgame is, **start by breaking it down into bits and pieces. Figure out what you have to do every week or every month to meet that goal.** It sounds hard to make a million dollars a year, but that's only $19,178 a week. **Break it down even further into a daily figure if you have to:** that's $2,739 a day for a seven-day week. It's still a lot, but it's a lot less than a million, isn't it?

That's just the financial side of your business, but **it also applies to who you're trying to serve.** Ask yourself: What do you have to do? What end result are you trying to reach? What's your overall plan? **Then, go backwards from there and figure out how to get there.** It's just like planning a trip. It's not often that you just take off down the road and end up somewhere; usually, you make plans on exactly how you're going to get there, using what roads, and where you're going to stop for the night. You have to start by saying to yourself,

"Okay, I'm going from Point A to Point C," and then you have to figure out where Point B is in the middle, and how that's going to get you to your end destination. It's the same thing in business. **First you figure out where you're going, where you want to be in the end, and then figure out the route to get there.** It's a basic point, but it's one I think we can definitely stand to hear over and over again.

That said, it's most important to have a general idea of your endpoint without worrying where you'll buy gas and where the rest stops are along the way. **Everyone focuses on the details way too much. The fact is, the concept itself is more important than the details. The details will come, but the concept comes first.** That's probably one of the top five most important things I have to teach you. Recently, our company set some very high sales goals that we've never been able to break. We decided that was going to be our goal: to make a certain amount of sales every single month. We've come close a bunch of times, but we've never actually hit that goal, and certainly we've never come close on a consistent basis. But through the process of setting this very high goal — which some people would call foolish or impossible — we've created some sound ideas and strategies. The ideas are becoming clearer every single day as we work towards this goal. Had we not sat down and said, "What's it going to take to do "X" amount of money every single month to hit our goals?", we would never have come up with these ideas.

The best ideas, the best breakthroughs, come in the muddy process of actually doing the biggest and best things. You don't have to have every detail in line before you start: you start toward your destination, whether you intend to make a million bucks or you're planning that sweet family vacation in Orlando. The details come once you've set the destination.

Let me give you a few specifics on this particular topic. A

few weeks back, I asked myself this question: "What would it take for us to do $20 million a year in sales?" A little voice came back that said, "Well, if you had 2,000 people who gave you ten grand apiece, you'd have your $20 million." Then another little voice said, "Well, what do we have to do to get 2,000 people to give us $10,000 each?" (Believe me, it's not that I'm a lunatic here — I'm talking back and forth to myself!) That other voice comes back and says, "You need a package that sells for $10,000." Then the first voice says, "What kind of package can you sell for $10,000 that would be so phenomenally successful that people couldn't even control themselves, so that 4,000 would gladly give you $10,000 each in one year?" All of a sudden light bulbs came on and fireworks started exploding, and I began to put ideas together.

I'm not trying to pretend that this process will automatically create fantastic ideas, but it sure helps the process along. **Ideas come to you when you start this process of "what if." "What if" thinking is important because it opens up possibilities.** You're thinking you want to reach a certain goal; so what do you have to do to accomplish it? All of a sudden you start thinking, "What if I did this, or what if I did that? What if I created this? Instead of having a package with this stuff in it, what if I kept adding stuff to make the value overwhelming, so people just couldn't refuse?" That's what you need: an offer too good to refuse. So ask yourself good questions because that's how you'll get good answers. Nothing is as powerful in this context as asking yourself, "What if?" **Each of your answers will lead to another question.** It's a great way to brainstorm.

Sadly, a lot of people I've talked to ask themselves bad questions. Oh sure, they certainly ask "what if" questions… but they say, "What if I start business and I fail? What if I start my business and someone sues me, or I send out this Direct-Mail campaign and nothing happens? What if my wife finds me buying all this mail order stuff?" None of those questions are going to help you in any way, shape, or form. You have to ask *positive* questions, like "What happens if I mail out this campaign and I get a million dollars? Where am I going to put my offices?" **You have to focus on the right questions, ones that push you in a positive direction.**

My fellow marketer and friend Don Bice talks about how, when he got started in marketing, you got into a joint venture with someone who's well known in the business. Don was all, "Gosh, what if I don't make enough money to cover my expenses? What if this doesn't work?" The man he was doing the joint ventures with had "what if" questions too, but they were entirely different. "What if I get more orders than I can process myself? What if I can't get a large enough quantity of these items? How do I deliver them?" Don's questions were all fear-based; **all of his partner's questions were searching. He wasn't worried about what happened if it went wrong. That's how you have to act.** It may not always work out, but if you have all the bases covered, you'll do just fine.

It's not always going to go the way you want it to; you'll just have to accept that Mr. Murphy is alive and well. You may get sued from time-to-time. Your wife (or husband) might get upset with some chance that you take. You know you're likely to fail sometimes. The taxman may come tomorrow. None of that can be an issue. **Here's what your attitude has to be: in spite of all the alligators, in spite of Murphy, in spite of the possibility of failure, and in spite of all that happens, you need to keep moving forward.** You're going to stay flexible, you're going to keep on doing different promotions, and you're going to push the heck out of the ones that really work. Success is quite easy if you recognize that there will always be alligators angling for you — but so what?

It all comes down to a belief in yourself, too. Most negative people aren't successful because they always think of what can go wrong first. If they think, "I'd like to make $10 million," the voice inside of them tells them, "You're crazy! You better think about trying to make $100!" They never think big. They're always negative, and they always feel inadequate. The big thinkers have to be celebrated because they think big, especially if they'll take action. Now, I've seen big thinkers who won't do a damn thing, and they never succeed either. But a big thinker who's willing to do some work and take positive action is hard to keep down.

CHAPTER FIFTEEN

Stop putting out brushfires!

The average small business person spends most of their day putting out brushfires. Their time and energy get zapped by all the minor problems that come up from day to day, and they're never able to pull back and work on their business. That is to say, "There's no real game plan or strategy."

You can't make this mistake. Instead you must be like the architect of your building, not the building manager. I think that's a useful analogy. Think about it: you have to focus on your strengths. You have to focus on game plan, which is all about making more sales and profits. You have to realize that no company ever went out of business because they had too many sales and too many profits — unless the government put them out of business. Companies go out of business because their sales and profits suck; they're just not making enough money so, after trying to struggle and scrape along, they finally get out. The pain becomes too great, or their creditors start coming after them, or whatever. **What you need to do is focus on your profits.** That's your game plan. You have other people to fill in on all the other areas; you have to develop a team.

I really do believe that some entrepreneurs can do anything. I think there's something to be said for knowing how to do everything within your company. I also believe in developing a team, and putting other people to work handling all of the stuff that gets in your way that other people can do for you. That doesn't necessarily mean employees, either. There are services on the Internet where you can find all kinds of people around the world, working right out of their homes, who'll do a wide variety of work for you. Some marketers have small armies of these little entrepreneurs working for them, so they don't have to pay taxes and all that confusing stuff. Even better, **they've created a situation so that the maximum amount of their time and energy can be devoted to building more sales and more profits.**

Here is another powerful point along the same lines: **Every day, you should strive to get one thing done that can lead to more sales and profits in your business.** There are a lot of entrepreneurs who are always doing things, but they never get things done. Just set a goal every day that, come Hell or high water, you're going to get something done that contributes to sales and profits in the future. Think about that. You may have projects you're working on that take you weeks and months to actually complete, but every day you're actually getting one thing done. That's 365 days for those of us who work seven days a week — 365 different things we can get done every day that contribute to our bottom line.

It's too easy to get sidetracked putting out fires. You can get so bogged down taking care of those problems instead of moving you toward your goals that you *have* to set aside a period of time every day that's devoted to nothing but moving you toward those goals. **You've got to spend a significant amount of time planning how you're going to reach your goals.** You don't need to spend your whole life planning, but you need to plan where you're going and how you're going to get there — or all that activity spent putting out all the fires is for no purpose whatsoever. A key point in finding time for planning, as boring as you may think it is, is getting people to do mundane things for you.

Some small business people feel they can't really afford

outside help. **The solution is that they should think about what they can do to work *on* their business.** For example, getting up in the morning and spending an hour thinking about what they can do to make their business more profitable and productive, before they actually start all the little tasks they have to take care of. Then, as soon as they start making some money, they can get those outside, independent contractors to handle stuff for them, so they can put more effort and time into making their business successful.

Dan Kennedy is a good example of this. He's phenomenally successful, but he still makes sure he spends time everyday working on his business. He tells himself, "I'm going to get up and write an hour and a half before I do anything else." Now, that's real slick if his first appointment is at 11:00, but he has the discipline to set the clock an hour and a half earlier even if his first appointment happens to be at 7:00 a.m. and he has to travel for an hour to get there. **I think this willingness to work on the business is a trait of all successful entrepreneurs.** Think about this. First of all, you've made progress every day. Second of all, you're free after that — because you've done what you had to do.

The secret is to see your business as a whole, and try to think like a general would. You never see the general on the front line; he can't afford to be there. He's too valuable to the war effort. The same concept is true for our businesses. **We're too damned valuable to do the grunt-work that other people can do.** Oh, being the general of your business doesn't make you any better than anybody, **it just has to do with where you're planning to take your business.** Every hour you spend doing trivial work is time wasted, at least if it's something someone else can do. **Focus on the things that contribute to your bottom line.**

CHAPTER SIXTEEN

The Magic Pill, Part 2.

We're back to the magic pill again! Remember, people are looking for and willing to spend a ton of money for a magic pill in *any* market. The magic pill is very important because most of us forget that people don't want what we have for sale. They really don't. **They want the *benefit* we can offer them. So start with that benefit first, then build the product and offer around it.**

Let's take a look at the ingredients of that magic pill, and discover what we can put in it to make it as attractive as possible to the potential customer.

First of all, **we want a pill that accomplishes the benefit effortlessly.** That's is very important. Everyone wants to be rich, or at least have as much money as they desire, and they want it as quickly as possible. They want to get as much money as they can for the smallest expenditure of effort. We want to lose weight, but we want to do it without effort, without exercise. We want the fat to just melt away. A powerful headline is one that promises that benefit immediately, like "Lose weight without exercise." We want to master a skill effortlessly without pain and without failure. Whether it's Spanish or French, we want to learn it without studying. We just want to put a CD in the player and suddenly know it. A lot of education has been sold that way: insert the CD into your machine and master this material on the way to work. A few years ago, even learning while you slept was a popular idea. What could be more effortless than that?

Number Two: **we want to achieve the benefit quickly.**
Speed is a very important part of the magic pill. Not only
must it be effortless, but also it should happen quickly. The
faster, the better. We're an instant society. We used to wait
days for photos, then we got them in same day, and now we
get them in an hour. Now I see 45-minute photos advertised.
We want the benefit, and we want it in our hands
immediately. It hasn't been too many years ago that the ad
said, "Lose 10 pounds in 30 days!" Well, that's not fast
enough. Those were successful ads then, but now we want
ads that promise we can lose 10 pounds in 10 days. We want
the benefits in our hands *right now.*

The third component is **to increase the quantity of the
benefit.** In other words, **give your customers more results
for the same effort.** For a book on speed-reading, that might
be, "Double your reading speed in just seven days" or "Double
your power to learn." Always promise a larger benefit for the
same amount of effort.

The fourth component is guaranteed results. We all
want to think the magic pill we're looking at is guaranteed to
give us the results we want. Certainly we want to achieve
those results at the lowest possible price, but if the pill is
magic, low price isn't important.

I think those are the **key ingredients of that magic pill:
no effort, quick results, larger benefits.** These are so
powerful that you could chart the potential success of a
product by how close you get to the magic pill. The closer you
are, the more people are willing to pay for it. With a lot of
advertising, that's exactly what happens. They move toward
the magic pill until it gets to the point that it stretches our
credibility, and then we go back and start going another
direction, and we move toward the magic pill again.

So the magic pill is important for you to figure out.

Let's just take a quick example here, and go back to my mention of the headline "Lose 10 pounds in 30 days!" To make it stronger we might say, "Lose 10 pounds in the next 10 days!" That would do it, right? It promises the benefit faster. Then we can move closer to the magic pill. "Lose 10 pounds in the next 10 days without exercise!" That makes it stronger and closer to the pill. "Lose 10 pounds in the next 7 days without dieting, while you sleep!" That's even stronger, because we've shortened the time and reduced the effort. What could be easier? The next step might be "Lose 10 pounds in 7 days while you sleep — while eating anything you want!" Now, that's even better — but here's the danger. When we started getting really close to that magic pill, we start stretching that credibility, and there's a very fine line there — because what is the magic pill? In this dieting example, it's "Lose 10 pounds instantly in your sleep — tonight!" That's what they're really looking for, so we just have to get as close as we can and deliver. But we also need to know when to stop. **So look for headlines and titles and product benefits that come as close as is credible to being a magic pill, and your sales and your profits will both skyrocket.**

I've worried for years about hyping my products too much. It's been a major concern of mine. How close do you get to the whole magic side of the whole thing without it being too unrealistic? What we've tried to do — but not accomplished — is that whenever we have an offer that we feel gets real close to the magic pill, **we try to build tremendous credibility into the whole promotion so we can justify the hype.** We worry a lot about going over the top, but we hardly ever do. Because that's true, 80 percent of your message should be emotion, and only 20 percent intellect. People make their buying decisions on emotions, mostly — but when you tell someone they can lose 10 pounds in 7 days while they sleep and still eat like a pig, a good percentage are going to say, "This sounds so good, and this is just what I want, but I just don't believe this person!"

That's when **you need to provide an explanation for the intellect:** "this is possible because of A, B and C," and give very good A, B and C reasons because all they want is a little nudge to their intellect. **The rest of the buying decision will be due to their emotions.** You need a gimmick to give them a reason that it will happen: "It's because of this secret ingredient or ancient herb that has been added." <u>Give them some component that makes it happen, that gives them an explanation for the benefit</u>.

Be honest with your explanation, but also tell them the truth about it. My friend Ted Ciuba has an offer where he tells people, "You can earn a $1,000 per hour with this business opportunity!" Well, that's the truth — but you can't earn $40,000 a week in a normal business week. There's an asterisk right next to the offer that leads to a footnote that says, "Beware! These results refer to the time that you actually spend in doing these deals. This will likely be the average that you actually earn."

Disclaimers are important, and not just because you warned them. You see, people are skeptical when they read our materials. No matter how much they want to believe, there's another part of them that has gotten ripped off before. There's always that little voice in the back of their head that says, "Yeah, right!" You've got to address that little voice. That's the whole secret here.

As I've said, I often worry about going over the top, making it all too "hypey." In my opinion, **it's fine to make the first draft of your copy over the top.** In fact, I think it's a good idea; you just have to go back and tame it later. <u>When you edit, you can soften those claims and bring it more into line</u>. If you're holding back because you're afraid you're going over the top, what I fear you'll do is reduce the enthusiasm and excitement in your letter. **If you let all that out, and get that enthusiasm and excitement in your first draft, then you can go back and bring your claims more into line with what you think people will believe.** You can have a claim that's valid but still sounds unbelievable. Sometimes it's better to scale it back a little and make it sound a little more believable — even though you can deliver more than you're promising.

One other thing to remember when you're writing copy is to **try to predict the questions that are going to pop into your reader's mind.** For example, you should directly address the point about people believing that something's too good to be true. You can say, "Okay, I know by now that you're probably skeptical. You probably think this is too good to be true — but let me tell you exactly why it *is* true." Or maybe they're wondering, "How can they do this? How can they give me a $500 television for $10?" **So you answer that question.** You say, "By now you're probably wondering how in the heck we can offer this $500 television for $10. Let me explain. A whole big bunch of these fell off of a truck and we found them in a ditch, so now we're selling them to you for $10!" Don't ignore the questions in their heads. You don't pretend they're not going to ask — because they will. **What you need to do is come up with a reasonable, credible answer for any question they have.** If you can do that, if you can answer that question, then you've pulled them back into your letter. In some cases you don't have to worry about these big claims, as long as you have a story that makes them reasonable in your reader's mind.

Here's another simple but important point that all of us, as professionals, live by. We get into this state where we write these what I call "National Enquirer" headlines and copy — but we always come back and edit. **Never tell a lie, but don't be afraid to express your opinions. Just be honest.** For example, we have a promotion right now where we're telling our customers that the future's uncertain. We have a solid plan that this is going to bring in a million dollars a month for our company. There are no guarantees or promises, but that's our goal. We believe that this is the million-dollar-a-month plan for us, and you can cash in with us. The promise is out there, the allure that attracts new clients, **but we also make it clear that nothing is guaranteed.** <u>We've been careful to state our claim in a way that's balanced enough so that the customer will understand it, and won't think we're trying to fool them.</u>

CHAPTER SEVENTEEN

The greatest challenge of Direct-Mail Marketing, and how to overcome it and make huge sums of money.

The greatest challenge of **Direct-Mail is simply the fact that it's an advertising message carrier with no entertainment value.** This can make it harder to get people's attention, and here's an absolute truth: people want to be entertained. They want to see jugglers and dancers, people singing, and all that stuff. Most people in this country are like zombies who are hypnotized by their lives and they're just doing the same thing day after day. They get up and go to work. They have lunch and continue to work. They go home and sit in front of the television for a couple of hours. That's a little bit of entertainment, but they really zone out during television. They go to bed, and then they do it all over again. They're hypnotized.

A lot of people think, "Well, in this situation, it's going to be easy for me to sell, because people like mail. If I send it to them, they're going to read it." But that's not necessarily true. You have to realize, first of all, that **your message really has to stand out because people have other things competing for their attention.** They have television: it's piped into their house 24 hours a day, 365 days a year. They have more channels now than ever before. There's the telephone. There are FAX machines, and now there's the Internet, which is even bigger than cable television or even satellite television — and it's growing all the time. At the same time you're mailing them a sales letter, there are 5 or10 other companies doing that too on that exact same day. So you're saying, "Oh, my gosh. Direct-Mail marketing, I can't do that! It's an impossible task." **But it's *not* an impossible task — far from it.** What you have to do is ask yourself the right question: "How can I give them some entertainment value in this Direct-Mail piece? How can I separate myself from everything else? What can I do, or what five things can I do, what seven things can I do, what ten powerful things can I do to this Direct-Mail piece that's going to make them stop what they're doing and sit down with this letter and start to read it and get involved?"

There are several other things you can do to get people to read your letter. **First, consider the envelopes you mail it in.** You have to decide if it's going to be sneak-up mail: is it going to look like a Hallmark card that maybe Aunt Mary sent? Is it going to look like an official piece of mail from a lawyer or the IRS? Or is it going to be all junked up with teaser copy, giving the benefits that you know that they want because you have that targeted mailing list? **If you know their desires, you can hit them right off the bat on the envelope with that biggest desire and that biggest benefit.**

Another thing you can do is grabbers. If someone gets something in the mail that's kind of lumpy or bumpy, that piques their interest. Hey, maybe there's something of value in it! There can be a lot of different things in an envelope that can stimulate people's curiosity because all the other mail they're getting is Plain Jane ordinary mail. This one has something in it, so they want to open it up.

A third thing has to do with the letter. Once they've opened it up, **you can get their attention with all sorts of**

different fonts. You can have Times New Roman, and you can have Courier, and you can have Arial, and any of the hundreds of other different fonts that are available. **You can have bold highlighting or underlining,** and some of the fonts can be larger than others — as long as you break them from their hypnotized state with a little variation. If you have the entire letter — 8, 12, 24 pages or more — all in 10-point Courier with none of it bolded or underlined, you're just putting them right back into the trance state, and they'll go to something more exciting like watching a test pattern on TV.

Another thing you can do is **add pictures.** People love to look at pictures, so add them to your letter. **You can tell them stories.** You can give them **testimonials.** There are tons of different things that you can do, but you have to realize that with all the competition out there, with all the entertainment they have piped into their homes and as hypnotized as these people are, you have to ask yourself the question: *"What can I do to wipe all that other stuff away and put my Direct-Mail piece on the top of the pile and get their full attention?"* If you can answer that question, you've hit the key, and you can have a very successful Direct-Mail campaign that blows everything else away.

While it may go against your grain, **it's important to make that marketing piece as entertaining to the eye as possible.** Use different fonts, different colors, striking graphics. It also makes the mail stand out, and that's very important. This kind of design mixture entertains the eye and gets it excited, just like good copy gets the mind excited. There's one caution you need to take here: if you're selling upscale products to an upscale market, this tactic doesn't work well. Otherwise, it really does make a big difference.

We have a piece out there right now that's working great for us. It's this 17 x 22 poster that's folded down and then mailed in an 8 ½ x 11 format. I swear this piece is terrible looking! It's like a disaster. It has all these weird colors all over it, and the copy is ugly looking and irregular. The whole piece looks like a train wreck — and yet it's pulling. One of the reasons **it's pulling is because it looks different from anything out there in the mail stream.** We knew that people were either going to hate it or respond well to it; there was no middle ground. It was wild, it was crazy, it was loaded with all these odd features... I even included my whole family photograph, with my son-in-law and my daughter-in-law and my grandkids. I blew it up real huge, and put it all on there. Somebody who isn't familiar with our market would go, "What in the hell is this?"

But you see, it's not a train wreck for our market. **It violates a lot of good design rules, but content wise it's absolutely perfect — because it's establishing me as a real person.** The family picture says I'm a family man, and that I've been around awhile. It's all the things that are opposite of the anonymous corporate crap that comes out of New York or Chicago. Visually, it's also exciting, although it violates a lot of rules of visual layout. In marketing terms, it's packed with powerful principles.

What's important, too, is to realize that when people speak to each other, they usually do so informally, but most people make things a lot more formal when they write. It's good to get away from that because **the more we can talk to our prospects one-to-one, informally, the better, usually, the sales letter is.** Formal grammar and the things you're taught in college don't make a great sales letter. You have to try to talk to people in your communications the same way you'd talk to them if they were sitting just three feet away from you. Write so that your personality comes out on the page — so you sound like you're a real person. **Most people don't really want to do business with companies, they want to do business with other people.** I think that's especially true in Direct-Response Marketing, though maybe not retail so much.

One of the things that we've been doing lately is putting dollar bills in a lot of our mailings. **We get brand new, crisp, uncirculated one-dollar bills and we glue them onto our letters** with a special glue stick that uses the same kind of glue you get on Post-It notes. I even get phone calls — I swear this is true — from people apologizing because they didn't have the money to take us up on the offer but they felt guilty because we sent them a dollar! It's not like our switchboard's always lighting up with calls like these, but we've received them on more than one occasion. Now, we're going to take that idea one step further, and on our more expensive packages we're going to test $2 bills and $5 bills — and we're going to even test $10 bills on our very expensive packages.

Of course, we're going to test these very slowly. Only a fool would test 1,000 letters with $10 bills on them without testing 50 or 100 first — but we're thinking that if you put a $10 bill on a letter to your very best customer for a high-priced item, you're just going to shock them. And that's what you need to do: **you have to find a way to just wake them up and get their attention.** You have to find a way to wake them up and zap them. Jeff Gardner says that when he's writing these pieces, he's thinking of a mental cattle prod. What can he add to his letter that's going to be a cattle prod to zap the readers out of their trance, and get them to pay attention? After all, they have so much other stuff they could pay attention to. **If you don't zap them immediately and put your best offer at the end of the letter, if you make it bland and boring, then you've lost the game.** The game is making money. That's why we're in this business. You can't make that money if you can't get people involved in a letter — and you can't get them involved in a letter if there's not something that shocks them awake, that makes them *want* to become involved in the letter. You absolutely have to cut through the clutter and get their attention.

The relationship model.

If you're going to make more sales, **you're going to have to be believed** because people will buy from people they believe. My best advice is to think about how best to serve your customers, not to think about sales. **Think about the customer first.** *Thinking about sales is the wrong thinking.*

Your first task is **to think about what the customer wants.** This is something that I've talked about before, but I'm going to hammer on it again and again because I want you to know exactly what makes people buy and re-buy. **It's *building a relationship with your customers.* We have to be willing to spend money to keep in touch with our customers. If we're mailing, we want to mail to our customers again and again, as much as eight, ten, twelve times a year, so we're always on their minds. They're always thinking of us, because we're always thinking of them. We're making similar offers every time. We want to show a friendship with our customer.

In the past couple of years, I've started to send out a lot of Christmas cards to customers. A few years ago I would have said, "Oh, that's foolish. It's just added expense. You're not asking for any business, you're just saying, "Thanks for the business in the past, and here's a card." You're just showing friendship. But I realize how important it is now because when I first started sending Christmas cards a few years ago many people replied to me — and some even said this was the first time a marketer had ever sent them a Christmas card. Now, sometimes I cheat a little and I'll pop a card in with an order that's going out in December — but I always sign every card. If the cards are pre-printed, black on white on the inside and very colorful on the outside, then I'll sign with a blue pen. I want people to know it's personalized. **The more personal we can get with our customers, the more business we'll get.** I learned a long time ago that the best thing a marketer can do is to fall in love with their business. Don't fight it, just absolutely fall in love with your business. That means really falling in love with your customers because our customers make everything possible: the house that you own, the investments you have, the car you drive. Everything that comes to us comes to us from our customers, so, **we always want to convey the message that we really care about them.**

Sometimes customers call us up and gripe about something, or they didn't get this, or we forgot to put in a bonus or we did something wrong. There was a time that I considered this such a nuisance I'd tell my staff to take these calls if I could avoid them. Now I realize that when you have good customers spending good money with you, you have a responsibility to take those calls and satisfy those customers. Some marketers look down on their customers. The ones who have products and services that are inferior and know they're ripping off their customers don't feel good about themselves, and they think anyone that buys from them is a chump because the stuff they're selling is crap and if people are buying this crap, they're stupid. That's the wrong attitude. The right attitude is to be in love with our customers, to serve them well, and to give them more value than they paid for. So, **if we convey the message that we *really* care, that we *really* want to help, that we're very sincere about this, that we *really* want to serve and we want to do more for our customers than our competition, that we want to give them more benefits than anyone else and fulfill their desires and do it quickly — that's what people appreciate.** That's how you build a great business.

Too often, marketers are just thinking of the money that they hope to make, and don't want to take the time to have relationships with their customers; but really, **the relationship with the customer is what brings in the money.** Too many people are self-centered about what they're doing. They want to make $1 million a year, but they don't seem to realize that's only possible because of the people they do business with, and therefore they have to put those people on a pedestal and serve them well. **All their hopes and dreams come through serving the hopes and dreams of the customer.** As Zig Zigler said, you can get anything you want, but to do so you have to be willing to give others what *they* want. It's this constant level of service to people that enriches us.

That's where a lot of people miss the boat. First of all, you have to admit that nowhere in the conventional schooling system do they really teach anything about business, so it's not necessarily your fault if you don't see the real picture at first. Most people look at business as the one-time sell. They look at it as earning, let's say, a million dollars, which is a big goal. They don't even stop to think, "Hey, not only do I want to earn a million dollars, but I want to earn a million dollars every year for the next 10, 20, 30, or 40 years. **The only way to do that is to treat these people with the love and respect and appreciation that they deserve.** It just makes good business sense. **Sometimes the customers that give you the hardest time, the ones who are the biggest pains in the butt, are also the best customers.** As they teach you when you get into sales: when you go out and face prospects face-to-face, beware of the prospect who has no objections. Beware anytime a prospect agrees with everything you're saying. In the back of your head you're thinking, *I'm going to get this sale; this is the perfect prospect.* Actually, no: oftentimes the perfect prospect is just the opposite. They're the ones who are giving you the hardest time. They're grilling you on everything you say. They're making your life hell,

whereas even if you make the sale to the other people, they never stick. The ones who are giving you hell are doing so because they have real applications to think of. Will the product work this way for them? Will this or that apply in this or that circumstance? Whereas the people who are fuzzy about what they need just say, "Sounds good to me."

My friend Don Bice spent 30 years selling to corporations, and he had one rule: **if they don't object to the price, they're never going to buy.** When someone says, "Oh, money is no object in this. This is very important to us," the reason is because they have no intention of really buying. Don never found an exception over the years. Whenever he found a client who wasn't concerned about the price — whether it was a corporation like Disney or a small company — it was because they were not a serious buyer.

So objections are opportunities. When you talk to customers who have objections to your price, you learn what their concerns are. It's very interesting. As you spend time on the phone talking to customers, you can eventually go through the mailing list and come to names and hear the voices associated with them. They're real people, so when you sit down to write your sales material, it's much easier — because now you're writing to real people. You can think of at least one of those customers on your list.

So the key is to look at them as honest to goodness, flesh and blood people just like the ones you love the most! My friend Russ Von Hoelscher was recently telling me about a case where his company shipped an order to New York City by UPS. They didn't have the apartment number on it and it must have been a big apartment building because it came back to them. They didn't know what to do with it because they didn't have a phone number. Finally the customer called raising holy hell. Russ' secretary couldn't handle it, so she passed it on to him. Russ listened to the customer, and then he said as nicely as possible, "We're very sorry. We made a mistake. We didn't have your apartment number on there. You must be in a large building." The customer said it was 24 stories or something. All of a sudden, he was soothed down, as soon as Russ said they were wrong and had made a mistake and they were sorry for this delay. Then he customer got to talking to Russ, and Russ wrote up a new $295 order in the next five minutes! The point is, you need to be willing to take their fire, and then turn it into ice so you can make the sale.

Another thing you can do is try to program the word "problem" out of your vocabulary and replace it with "challenge." **With challenges come tons of opportunities.** A lot of people in Russ' position might have said, "Oh, I'm *never* going to talk to this person." You could write them off or send them a refund check instead. But in the challenge of the customer calling up and being very unhappy, there was the opportunity to get more money out of him by apologizing profusely, thereby possibly making him a better more long-term customer. It worked well in this case! When you're dealing with people, you have to realize that these are people just like you. If you've had problems with a phone company, or the gas service, or any other type of company, you wanted it handled not just the right way but in an even better way, right? **You want someone to go above and beyond; and if they do, you'll feel connected to that company.** Whenever you buy anything you'll want to buy from that company because you know if there's ever a problem, they're going to make sure that it's settled to your satisfaction.

You need to do that in your own business — no matter whether things are just swimming along, or whether there comes a challenge where someone isn't getting what they ordered when they thought they were getting it, or they were doubled charged or whatever. Look at the opportunity there. **Work to make them a better customer by going all out to**

make sure they're happy and satisfied. Even if you have to part ways, do it on good terms. Don't make any snide remarks, or say "Well, I'm glad to get rid of you, jerk," even if you are. End it in a great way, because you never know when they're going to be back, or how much money they're going to put in your pocket then.

Now, a lot of people have problems with refunds. I know that I did when we first started our business back in 1988. It made me *so* angry to get those packages back, and have people want to actually take us up on our guarantee! I used to just be so ticked off, but that just shows you what a fool I was. This is one area where I've changed my mind completely. Now, if anything, I'm a fool because I'm too liberal about refunds. If a customer calls and expresses any dissatisfaction, I'm the first one to say, "Okay, you'll get your money back, no problem." **We have the most liberal refund policy, maybe some people think it's too liberal.** But I remember a few years ago when we had a seminar where our customers spent a considerable amount of money to be there and I asked just on the spur of the moment, "Let's see a show of hands of everyone in this room who's ever ordered a product from our company and returned it for their money back." We had about 100 people in the room, and 7-10 hands that shot into the air right away. That made me feel damn good because that told me that I was right in my thinking about being liberal with refunds. **Just because they're not happy with one product doesn't mean they're not going to come back and buy from you again.**

Having said that, though, sometimes you can be too quick to make a refund. You can often ask the customer, "What would it take to make you happy?" They'll tell you something that's much less than a refund. They just want you to do something else, or make this good, or refund their postage, or something smaller. **Before you promise the moon it's really better to let a customer vent and learn**

what they're unhappy about. Don't do this when someone asks directly for a refund, of course, but otherwise hear them out. Maybe they're dissatisfied with the service or the postage, or didn't get what they were supposed to. Don't argue with them. Don't tell them they're wrong. Don't make excuses. Let them talk it out completely, and then when they've said their piece you say, "I'm very sorry. We'll do everything we can to make you happy. What would it take to make you happy?" Very often, just the fact that you listened and you gave them a chance to express their dissatisfaction is all they needed. **It's amazing how often the solution they want is a lot less than the solution that you may have granted them.**

CHAPTER NINETEEN

Your #1 goal as a marketer.

Your entire business has to be centered on getting each customer to give you the maximum amount of their money. While we talk about altruism and how we make our money by helping others, or by providing a valuable product or service, **the truth is that your ultimate goal in business is to make money.** It doesn't matter whether it's a retail business selling shirts and ties, or if it's a service business that sells a certain service, or if you're selling a business opportunity. It has to be profitable, or there's no point.

There are really only two reasons to be in business. **Your primary function is to serve your customers; your secondary function is to make a profit.** The way to make profits is by servicing your customers. You're in the business of making money. That's it. There's really no other reason that you should start a business. You might have seen a need, sure, but your ultimate goal is to find a market that needs to be served and to serve it, and therefore make a profit. It all comes back to the <u>ultimate goal of finding as many ways as possible to get your target market to give you as much of their money as possible</u>. When you think about it, it really is that simple.

But still, **you do have to serve your customers.** That's another reason you exist; there's no doubt about it, or at least there shouldn't be. But you can't stay in business unless you make money by serving them. This entire principle really isn't that difficult to grasp; I just wanted to make sure I reiterated it because I think it's very important. It goes back to what I've have been talking about: that is, the subject of **making the most money you can by starting with a market and knowing exactly what that market is, and who the people who make it up are.** Once you understand that, you can start going to that target market as often and as much as possible to try to get them to give you the maximum amount of their money. You want to suck as much money out of your target audience as possible; that may sound crude, but it's an effective and direct way of putting it. Obviously, making profits is what keeps you happy as an entrepreneur.

That said, a lot of companies just bypass this target altogether. **All too often, marketers don't even try to resell to customers who've bought one thing from them.** They never go back to the well, and that's a real mistake. My feeling is that they have this idea that the business of being in business is just making a little money from customers. However, **customers *want* additional products.** They want our attention. They want to give us more money, **so our focus should always be on getting the maximum amount of money from them.** That's selling them basic and deluxe packages, up-selling them on the telephone, giving them additional back-end offers, contacting them monthly or maybe even every two or three weeks. This is how you go about doing everything possible to get the maximum amount of money, not just getting a little bit of money and then ignoring them. Sure, I know this sound cynical and manipulative. But the fact is, if you're offering them products they can use, that have a direct benefit to them, then you're helping them even as you're helping yourself. You're doing nothing wrong, and they can always say "No" to whatever you put out there. In fact, most of them will. But they'll appreciate the offer.

When my mentor Russ Von Hoelscher first gave seminars with Al Galassco back in that day, they used to give a heck of a lot of them in Southern California, practically

---

every month: San Diego, Orange County, and Los Angeles especially. They worked with Dottie Walters, experienced and popular seminar leader and speaker and author, who joined them in some of the seminars. She'd always not only come there and give a speech, but she would also have all this product she sold in the back of the room. She told Russ and Al that they were cheating their customers by just putting on a seminar and giving away some seminar materials, but not having products to sell in the back of the room. Russ asked, "Cheating them?" And Dottie said, *"Yes, they want to take you home with them — so you should have books, manuals, tapes, and video, just like I do."* She used to sell a ton of them. He says he finally wised up to the fact that **this was the right thing to do because people *want more*.** Whatever they get, they want more of the same. **If you don't give them more, you've not only made a mistake that will cost you money, but you have actually cheated the customer.**

I think **a lot of entrepreneurs lose sight of the fact that their focus should be on maximizing their profits.** They spend way too much of their time doing the things that don't produce the largest amount of profit. My colleague Jeff Gardner has a sign on his wall that I've mentioned before: basically, it says, "Is what I'm doing right now worth $600 an hour?" He tells me the mantra's kind of stuck in his head, so he doesn't even look at the sign anymore. So whether he's, God forbid, scooping cat litter or talking on the phone with a customer or inputting something into the computer, his brain automatically says, "Is what I'm doing right now worth $600 an hour?" If his brain says, "No, it's only worth $5 or $10 an hour," he stops immediately and finds someone else to do it for him. That's exactly the route you should take when you're in business.

I know that for someone who's never made $600 an hour, that sounds a little unbelievable — but believe me, there are plenty of people using Direct-Response and

Internet marketing who make this kind of money and a lot more! They're involved in activities like writing sales copy and working on their promotions, and when you take the gross sales that they make on one promotion and the number of hours it actually took them to create some of the materials and ideas, well, they gross well over $600 an hour. I used to laugh at rich people who had chauffeurs and butlers and maids and people who took care of all of their stuff around the house. I used to think those people were just a bunch of egotistical freaks, and that they were in love with their power and were trying to be superior with everyone else. But I know better now. There are plenty of entrepreneurs who operate the same way. I know of a guy in Florida who's a copywriter. He rides around in a chauffeured limousine all day. When I first heard about that I thought, "What a self-righteous, self-absorbed, egotistical monster, to have someone drive him around in a limousine." Then I found out that most of the time he's riding in the back of his limousine, he's actually writing copy. Now I understood him.

And speaking of **focus,** notice that on this point, I didn't say that the whole goal is centered around getting as many people in the world as possible to give us money. **I said *each customer*.** Those are the people who are predisposed to give you money because they've already bought what you have and are most likely to buy more.

CHAPTER TWENTY

The insatiability of the marketplace.

People in most marketplaces tend to be insatiable, and thank God for that — because we can keep coming up with new stuff to sell them! For example, take the weight loss market. People don't just buy one thing when they get serious about losing weight: nope, they buy everything they can get. They go to Amazon.com and order five or ten books. They go to Weight Watchers. They go to Jenny Craig. They watch exercise shows and infomercials on television. They buy videos. They get exercise equipment. They're *insatiable.* You'd think a lot of the programs they're buying don't work, but usually it's the *person* that isn't working. You'd think that this would ultimately turn them off, wouldn't you? But it doesn't **because they've never gotten the benefit they wanted. That's why they're insatiable. They'll continue to purchase until they get that benefit.** Even if they *never* get that benefit, they may keep purchasing. Now, there are peaks and valleys in their patterns of purchasing; sometimes people lose the ability to purchase as much as they want, or go through periods of greater and lower interest. But if someone really has that desire and they really want that benefit, they'll continue to buy and buy and buy.

There are three great points that I would like to bring up here about people being insatiable. **Number One is back-end sales.** If people weren't insatiable, if you could make them satisfied with just that one product, our job would be so much tougher because we'd have to constantly be going out and getting new customers all the time. That's expensive. **Most, if not all, of the profits come from those back-end sales.** A lot of companies are willing to break even or lose money getting the customer in through that first front-end purchase, in the hopes of making all their profits through the back end purchases later. If people weren't insatiable, a lot of these companies would go out of business because there would be no back end sales. The person would get the product and say, "That's exactly what I'm looking for!" and they'd be done. <u>Thank goodness people are insatiable because once they get that first product you know they're going to be coming back for number two, number three, number four, and number five</u>.

That's my first point. **The second point is you need to continue to send your customers promotional literature.** People are insatiable, so they'll buy back end products, but that doesn't ultimately mean that companies will continue to sell. We talked about this previously — about how some of these companies just send one thing, and then they're done. They don't go back to their customers; they continue to try and get new customers all the time. Well, you need to contact your customers because they're insatiable. If you don't make them new offers — they <u>will</u> buy from your competitors. **For every month you're not mailing to your mailing list, that list is losing ten percent of its value.** You need to continue contacting your customers again and again, if only to keep up that relationship and maintain the value of that list.

The third point hits on competition because a lot of people come into any business and say to themselves, "There are so many people already in this business. How am I going to make a dime?" If you're looking at it that way, you're looking at it completely backwards! I would *never* want to be in a business that nobody else was in. **Seeing an empty market doesn't tell me it's an untapped market: it tells**

me that there's no desire, no need, and no want in that market. What I want to do is come into a market where there are already five, or 10, or 20, or 50, or 100 super-successful businesses because what that tells me is that the market is so insatiable they it can support all those companies. I know that I'm selling to a market that's so insatiable that there's room for Company Number 101 if I'm willing to offer an equal or better product or service value.

Those three points are important because **understanding that your customers are insatiable gives you an idea of how you can make long-term cash from your mailing list without having to beat yourself up to get new customers all the time.** Here's a good example of that, and it's a personal one. I've been reading and listening to all this motivational self-help stuff for about twenty years. I have tapes that go back from twenty years ago that I still listen to. I'm not exaggerating here — I probably have 10,000 or 12,000 cassette tapes, if not more. Do you think I'm going to stop? Of course not. I'm hooked. I'm an addict. Even though I've 12,000 cassette tapes, I'm going to buy some more next week. I'm a junkie! I'm addicted! Many of my friends are the same way.

Take my son-in-law Chris Lakey, an excellent marketer in his own right. He was telling me recently that even though he's in his mid 30's, he still enjoys sitting down and playing a good video game. He keeps buying them, even though he has a bunch of them he never plays. If he sees one that captures his interest, he'll buy it. I think it's the same thing with movie lovers, readers, and the like. Any time anyone has a certain desire, there's no stopping them until that desire is filled. **In many cases, it's *never* going to be filled, so they'll keep buying more and more of the same stuff that they've already bought.**

That's why a lot of us are junkies on marketing. When

something new comes out about marketing, I've got to have it — because if there's just one or two pearls of wisdom in the entire book or manual or tape that I haven't encountered before, then I feel I've gotten my money back many times over. <u>Sometimes I've taken one principle from a course or book and turned it into hundreds of thousands of dollars</u>.

So, when you're a junkie, you're a junkie! It doesn't matter whether it's gambling or diet books, it's marketing books or video games — **it's an insatiable desire that people will pay good money to fulfill again and again.** Some people even have a desire for something as mundane as fishing tackle. It's true! A fly fisherman I know never stops buying new lures and new tackle.

Here's another example: earlier, I mentioned something that happened to my colleague Ted Ciuba. He had a customer who came into their funnel with a $497 order and nine orders later — in less than two months — he'd purchased $5,943. Well, Ted was telling me, a few days ago as I'm writing this, that the same guy came through and ordered another product for $960. So in less than three months, the same customer spent $6,903 on Ted's products — and I'll bet you he buys the next offer Ted makes. Ted tells me that he happens to know that this guy buys from his competitors, too — so who knows how much he's spent this year on the same kinds of products! Now, that's insatiable.

However, the competition is one thing that a lot of our customers just can't get past. **We sell marketing and informational products that they use to draw in clients of their own.** When they see a crowded marketplace, they get concerned about all the competition. What you need to do is put them in the shoes of their own customer; tell them what I've just told you in this chapter. These companies wouldn't all be around for five, ten, fifteen, twenty years if the market wasn't insatiable, and people weren't buying from all sorts of different companies. That appeases some of them.

For the rest, you have to point out, "Let's look at yourself. Over the last six months or a year, how many of these different companies have you purchased from?" Then they think and they say, "Well, maybe 20 or 30." I say, "Well, hold it. That first time you purchased that money-making product, you weren't happy or satisfied?" They say, "Oh, I was satisfied, but I still wanted more information." I ask, "What did you do then?" They say, "Well, I got this letter in the mail, and I bought from it, and then I went to the magazine and I bought five or six things from there, and then I went to this seminar and I bought two packages from there, and I saw this infomercial and I bought three packages." I say, "Okay, you're proving my point. If there were any problem with competition, you wouldn't have bought from all of those companies. **What these companies are doing is feeding your desire and wants.** Having all these people in the market is good because it's feeding your needs and making you a better buyer because now you have so many sources, you want to buy from this company and this company and this company. I wouldn't worry about competition. **What I would worry about is getting your product out to these people as fast as possible, because they're hungry."**

Most of us talk to our best customers personally on at least a semi-regular basis, and sometimes they just amaze you. My friend Russ von Hoelscher was recently telling me about a time when he was talking to a customer of his, and he thought, "Gosh, she's bought so much product from me I don't think I'll even mention anything new. We have this new grand slam offer, but she's already spent thousands of dollars in the past year." Then she started telling Russ about all the things she's bought from my wife Eileen and I, and Jeff Gardner, and Ted Ciuba, too. That's the kind of thing that makes you realize that when they're buyers, they're buyers! **They're going to buy a lot of stuff from a lot of people, so keep sending**

them offers and keep telling them about new offers.

The very act of buying satisfies something within most people. Look at weight-loss: that's probably the best example. There are plenty of weight-loss systems on the market — and all you have to do is read the tabloids every week to know there are a lot of people in the business of providing them, too. That's because there are people who buy a new weight-loss gizmo or system every month. They're still heavier than they like, so obviously it's not working. But the thing is, just by buying that weight-loss goop, or pills, or whatever the latest no-work magic gimmick is, satiates a part of them — or at least it makes them feel like they're on their way to losing weight for sure. It gives them a little hope. They just keep buying and buying because the very act of buying sort of makes them feel like they're accomplishing something.

Now, a lot of people will look at that and ask, "How can you sell weight-loss products that you know won't be used by 98-99% of the people who by them?" I respond with two things. First of all, the point I've just mentioned: **in many cases, these people want to feel like they're doing something, like they're taking action.** Sure, actually doing the workout or using the materials is too much pain for them; it's above and beyond their comfort zone. By the same token, just sitting back and realizing, "Hey, I'm always going to be fat," is also too much pain — so they pick a middle ground. **That middle ground is taking action to buy the tapes or the workout equipment or the pills, even if they don't do anything with it.**

The second point I make is this: look, we can't be responsible for forcing them to use the product that way they're supposed to. **As long as we're delivering a great product that can actually deliver upon its promise if put into action, that's all we're responsible for.** We can't go to their home and sit them down into that little ab-rocker thing

---

and then start rocking them and saying, "Come on, rock some more! Ten more!" We don't have that responsibility. That's what personal trainers are for. Our responsibility is to deliver the best products possible to the targeted market, and let them take it from there.

Having said that, you can't be too critical of people who buy stuff and don't do much with it. Russ talked to a gentleman in Pennsylvania about a month ago. He told Russ that for over ten years, he's been buying Russ' books and manuals and tapes. He's also bought from Eileen and I, and Jeff Gardner, and Tyler Hicks, too. He told Russ that it took him ten years to finally crack open some of these things and really read them and listen to the tapes. Now he's started a business that's doing very well. You see? **You never know what's going to happen when someone's buying informational products.** They may just accumulate it and put it on the shelf — and then nine or ten years later, they decide to really do something. Different strokes for different folks.

I'm a pretty good example of that. For the last 20 years, I've been reading all kinds of motivational stuff, and listening to all the tapes in the world. Some of the principles, like goal-setting, I've been hearing over and over again for 20 years. Sometimes I think, "The next time I hear something about goal-setting, I'm going to puke." But after 20 years of listening to it until it just drove me crazy, I'm now actually doing something. I think some of us are either so stubborn or hard-headed that something like this takes 20 years of pounding to finally sink in!

CHAPTER TWENTY-ONE

The structure of a powerful, productive, hard-hitting sales letter.

Here's a simple six-step formula for writing powerful sales letters that can make you a fortune:

1. Start with a big promise.

2. Paint the picture.

3. Give them proof.

4. Tell them why it's unique.

5. Close by telling them that they must act now.

6. Make a very special offer if they do respond now.

Simple, right? So let's break these down. **The big promise should be your biggest benefit: the biggest one you can offer.** Put it in your headline, not just in ads but also in sales letters. **Next, paint the picture.** This is where we tell our story. **Pile on the benefits and build a tidal wave of desire for the product or service you're offering. This is crucial.**

Number three: **give them the proof your product works.** If you're selling a money-making plan, tell them exactly how much money they can expect to make. If you made $137,212.23, tell them that exact figure. Don't just say things like, "You can make $100,000 with this plan." **Tell them exactly what you've done yourself. Next, tell them why it's unique.** Try to create a USP, a Unique Selling Position for your product or service. You do this by highlighting the most important things about your product or service, telling them why your offer is better than anyone else's.

Next is Number Five: **close by telling them that they must act now.** People are lazy, and they'll put off til tomorrow what they should do today. We need to give them a good reason to take action. I found that **it's a good idea to give them an exact date when they must respond to get the special offer at the special price.** If they do respond quickly, hit them with a special benefit for taking action. That can be a quick reply bonus, where we give them some other gadget or gizmo or book or tape as a free bonus, or even several reports and tapes if they will act right now.

Actually there's a number seven, which is: **end with a reminder of your promise, a summary of your offer, and a strong call to action. This is where your "P.S." comes in.** Always use a postscript that capitalizes your offer. Years ago, I used to have an order form that pretty much stated what they were getting and the price, with room for their name and city, state and zip code. Now I use the order form as a selling vehicle, and I put some of the benefits on the order form. It works much better.

The key point here, I think, is to **make people realize that your product is unique and what the great benefits are.** If you're selling perfume, it's okay to mention that you're giving them two precious ounces in a designer bottle. You may even explain that 280 flowers had to be crushed to go into the perfume. But what people really want to know is what this fragrance is going to do for them. You have to tell a woman how beautiful she'll feel, how beautiful she'll smell, how she'll attract other people, how people will come to her because she's wearing this very exotic fragrance. **I always sell not just the obvious benefits, but also the real emotional benefits that people buy from.**

Formulas like this are an excellent shortcut in any marketing endeavor. You need a template or a formula for everything you do because you can take one offer that's been very successful and change the wording a little, plug in the new product or service — and find that the new promotion is just as successful as one you did a year ago. It's amazing. **Once you have a successful sales letter you can use that letter for all kinds of different products or services, just by making a few changes here and there.**

There's a famous copywriter who just lives about an hour from my friend Jeff Gardner, in Denton, Texas. He's famous for writing the exact same sales letter for every one of his clients — but he's very successful, meaning his sales copy actually works, so people keep hiring him. We call him the Letter Doctor. Once you know his sales letter, you could put one in a row of 20 different letters and you could pick out exactly which one is his because it's easily recognizable. This is a compliment to him, not a criticism. **We mailed one of his pieces, and it was our control for three years.** He makes more money than you'd expect, despite the fact that he tends to work pretty cheap. It's really not that cheap, though, because he can do things so quickly. He has the formula just like the one I laid out earlier.

That's what it takes: a successful formula that you repeat over and over. As you learn new things, you can plug in some new benefits and concepts to get people excited. The key to making a lot of money comes down to this: **you have to make people just salivate with desire.** You have to make them so desirous for your service or product that they just can't wait to get on the telephone or to get to the mailbox. They have to have it. They want it now. They might even tell you they'll pay extra for overnight delivery because they *have to have it.* **When you can write copy like that, you can get rich!**

Now, beware: this usually doesn't happen overnight. My mentor, Russ, has been doing it for 30 years. If you're reading this and just don't have these skills yet, you've got a couple of options. You can hire someone who does, or you just keep working and writing and plugging at it until you can do it in your sleep. Once I'd honed my skills, my very first sales letter was an instant success. Right before I wrote that first sales letter, I learned that there's a formula that will predispose your effort to success. It isn't getting your commas in the right place, or your question marks inside the quote marks! It's much more than that. It's what we've already talked about: **it's starting with your big league benefit in your headline, and maybe putting some sub-headings in, or making the offer with a take-away.** You know: "You better hurry. There's only a limited number!" When you follow that, it's just regular English that can, in fact, be very successful.

Most people are just too worried about writing. Well, one thing that I've noticed over the years: if you have a really great, irresistible offer, you may be able to get away with not having the best sales letter writing skills in the world. I can't say this will get you out of being able to write at some level, but it can help. For example, let's say that you had an unlimited supply of $100 bills that didn't cost you anything, and you were selling them for $1 each. How good of a sales letter would you have to write to make a whole ton of money? That's a great offer. Of course you do need to study how to write great sales letters, but the one thing I'd start doing before writing word one is to sit down and ask yourself, *"How can I make this an irresistible offer? What can I add, how can I tweak it, what can I change to make this an irresistible offer? Can I drop the price down by 10 percent, or can I give it away completely free? What can you throw in to make it even better?"* If you start with a hot offer, an offer people are going to salivate over, you don't have to be the world's greatest copywriter to make tons of sales.

Another key point is how excited you are, and how much enthusiasm you can get across in your letter. You need to get so excited about it that you think to yourself, "Man, this is what I'd wish I had if I didn't already have it!" There are people like this in every profession, people who are so enthused by what they're selling that their enthusiasm bubbles over into their writing. I know restaurateurs who do this: they write great sales letters because they really believe their food is absolutely the best, or that the environment they create in their restaurant really is conducive to romance between a couple. I saw a guy the other day who was selling decks — the kind you build onto the outside of your house. He has a little spiel where he talks about his certification and how he's been doing this for 21 years, and how he's developed six different breakthroughs. The guy really appreciates it, so you as the client or prospect are thinking, "Wow, this has to be good!"

And let me remind you: **you don't have to be all that good of a writer if you have a powerful offer.** Then too, <u>you don't have to be that good if you're already selling to your own customers</u>. I'm talking about people you have a relationship with, who have bought from you in the past. It becomes even easier to sell to them because the trust level they have for you means the response is generally going to be quadruple or better over a list of cold prospects who haven't ever done business with you.

All this really does keep coming back to the structure of a powerful, hard-hitting sales letter. **You don't have to be perfect; you don't have to even be great if you follow the outline I laid out at the beginning of this marketing**

secret. This is especially the case if you have a powerful offer. Each of the seven things I covered is a piece of a jigsaw puzzle that then you just connect together — and have your promotion right there. This all works much better when you have a list to mail to. But if you're just starting out and don't have a mailing list, or you can't afford one, there are still things you can do. Think about making some low-price offers, or even free offers, and overwhelm your potential customers! Make them think, "Wow, if I got this for $10 or if I got that for free, imagine how much the back-end offer is worth if I just go ahead and order it!"

A lot of business people never really think that way, though. They get involved with distributorships that are very expensive on the front end, and they're going out to people who have never heard of them. Often they use very poor judgment, too. I just received a mailing yesterday that used "Mr. & Mrs. Joe and Martha Johnson" as the name of their company. You don't want to mail to someone saying you're Mr. & Mrs. Joe and Martha Johnson. **You want to use a company name, even if you're starting out.** Sure, Joe Karbo was able to use his own name, but most of us want to use a company name to give an illusion that we're bigger than we are.

CHAPTER TWENTY-TWO

Work smart. Find the ways and means to revamp all of your successful material.

You have to find as many ways as you can to steal the hottest ideas that others are using in their marketing. This is one of the most powerful principles I know of when it comes to creating new offers for your customers. **There's a saying that says that nothing is new — there are only new ways of presenting old ideas.** That's powerful because it reminds you that there's no need to go out there and reinvent the wheel. Chances are, if a good idea comes to you, it's already been thought of by someone else.

So instead of focusing on finding new ideas, **focus on finding the best ideas other people are using, and incorporating those ideas in to your own marketing plan.** You might have a worry that "stealing," as we call it, might not be the right thing to do. But you're not stealing: you're just making use of existing ideas. If you look back to where that person got that idea, you'll probably find they probably got it from someone else, who got it from someone else, who can't even remember where they got it. Everybody shares ideas — you should do it, too.

Take General Motors and Ford, for example. Whenever one of them comes up with a new hot car model you can bet the other one will come out with something that looks very

---

similar within the next few months. Now, one of them has the GM logo on it and the other one has Ford on it, but they look alike because one of them took the other's plan and tweaked it a little. In some cases, they even build the new car on the same manufacturing line their competitor uses!

I mentioned earlier ago that my colleague, Chris Lakey, happens to like video games. Recently Microsoft and Nintendo came out with two brand new games that were almost exactly alike. It's no coincidence that both these video game systems came onto the market within the same week. One of them was in secret meetings, coming up with a new hot idea for a video game system, and somehow the other company found out about it — and they quickly put together their own, very similar, video game system. Both use new technology. **They take each idea that the other uses, and they incorporate their own versions in the new product.** Perfumers do the same thing. Cosmetic companies do, too — they usually come out with things very similar to something that's already on the market. **So there's simply no need to reinvent the wheel.** These companies have figured it out. It's something *you* need to figure out as well.

You must revamp your own sales material. This is very important. **If you've already written a great sales letter or created a great offer, you can simply rewrite it and turn it into an entirely different offer.** I'm giving away a real insiders' secret here because it's something that we all do. When we create a new offer — let's say we've written this great sales letter that's maybe 24 or 30 pages long — it may seem to someone who isn't in our business that we've labored for hours and hours. A lot of times we do, don't get me wrong — but we usually don't draw up a new, lengthy sales letter every time. Often it's a matter of taking an old offer and revamping it, or throwing some new stuff in with some old stuff. You can take entire paragraphs from old sales letters, or sometimes you can just take a line or even a phrase. You can do it with your guarantee, for example, if you've used a good guarantee before. Maybe you have a new offer that tells people how to make big money on the Internet, and you ran another offer, say six months or a year ago, that's on the same subject. You might be able to use a large block of copy from your old offer in the new offer. The same sales copy that applied then can apply now.

I want to share one idea that's has meant a lot to me over the years. That's **the concept of the swipe file — a place where you keep other people's ads and sales letters.** I started doing that from Day One. When I first heard about that concept I thought, "This is a powerful strategy. I'm going to save every piece of junk mail that comes to me and try and get on all these mailing lists by sending away for information. Then I'm going to keep this massive swipe file." Well, what ended up happening over a period of ten years is that I ended up with a whole huge room that was filled with this stuff. Have you seen those shows where they go into someone's house and they have newspapers and junk everywhere, and there's a little path carved in the room? That's what my swipe file room started looking like after ten years. So last year I ordered a great big Dumpster brought out to the house. It was one of those big construction Dumpsters they leave on construction sites, and a huge semi truck had to bring it out there. I took all of my swipe file crap and threw it away. Now I've been trying to do it more intelligently.

The second point is that even when you do use your swipe file, you have to allow yourself plenty of time to work on the promotion. You have to ease up a little bit on yourself. **When it comes time for the final editing stage, I'll spend a couple days going through my swipe file and seeing what little tidbits other people have used that I can throw into my own offer.** When I'm on my final rewrite, that's when I'll take out one of Jeff Gardner's sales letters, or one of Russ Hoelscher's or Ted Ciuba's or Don Bice's and say, "Hey, that was a really great idea!" Then I'll steal it!

Here is what I've found that works. I went to Office Depot and I bought two huge record books. They're about 300-400 pages each. I go through the sales letters I get, and if one's a really good letter that I know is going to make money, I usually cut out the first page and paste it in the book. Then I quickly go through the sales letter, and if I see any descriptions or words that I like I might cut them out and tape them to a page. Ever since I've done this, I've had a swipe file that makes sense — because once you have 1,000 sales letters that you're trying to keep in some type of box, they eventually become worthless because at some point the boxes get put in the garage and you never use them.

Here's another tip: **get a book called *Words That Sell.*** It's inexpensive, costing less than $15. That book is full of descriptions and exciting action words and ideas for headlines and more. It's a white paperback manual you can find at most bookstores or Amazon.com. This book will help you immensely.

One thing that I mentioned earlier is that most sales letters are written piecemeal. They're written in chunks, and sometimes they're made up of pieces of other letters that just keep getting rewritten over and over. There's a lot of cutting and pasting involved. Although everybody tries to give their sales letters the appearance of a friendly, informal letter they just sat down and wrote out quickly, the truth is that some people spend weeks and even months writing one letter — even when they're taking pieces out of an existing letter and rewriting them. We'd all like to dash them off, but depending on where you are mentally, getting a letter right can take a long time. We've all sat down at the computer after doing a couple weeks of research and literally tried to pound it out of our heads for a long time before something clicked. Then, in other cases, we sit down at the computer and boom! Sixteen pages flows out in no time. It's not necessarily consistent. That said, **the real key, no matter what you do, is trying to make it seem like you just sat down and wrote a one-on-one letter to somebody else,** whether that letter really took five minutes or a month — and believe me, it sometimes takes months to do it right.

The point is, you need to revamp your successful sales material. Remember: the keyword here is *successful*. When he talks about stealing from others with your swipe file, he says to use the hottest ideas others are using. **You want to put together both their successful ideas and yours.** When you do that, you end up with the very best and most significant elements of what's has already been proven to effective. Why would you *not* model what's already working?

So you're only looking for the best of the best. At our company, M.O.R.E., Inc., we've only had a few sales letters that have been anything near what I would call a "grand slam," to use a baseball term. Most of our offers are just base hits where we've made it to first base, or second if we're lucky. Sometimes we've had triples, but we've had few offers that quality as either home runs or grand slams. **We strive to use the elements from those grand slams in as many ways as possible** — in fact, we try to incorporate them into every other sales letter. We do that even when we're not certain what was such a hit. Sometimes you don't really know exactly why something worked as well as it did. You know it worked because the money came in and you have the results to prove it — but it's hard to really figure out exactly what made it click. Since you want to avoid reinventing the wheel as much as possible, **you take those very successful promotions and just try and rewrite them a little bit,** hoping and praying that something in that combination you've rewritten it's going to produce the same magic in terms of sales and profits as it did the first time. Sometimes it works, often it doesn't.

So remember: **a large part of constructing good offers is cutting and pasting, folks.** Even the top copywriters in the world, the guys getting paid huge amounts of money to write these sales letters — they're cutting and pasting, too, putting a little new stuff here and a little there. I find this fascinating and instructive, considering their obvious success. In any case, it's a lot easier now that we have computers to work with. When I first learned how to do this I didn't use a computer at all. One of my first sales letters I still have somewhere in my house; it was just a bunch of legal pads cut and pasted together, and it was like a great, big toilet paper roll. I'd spread it all out on the floor and I would cut and paste with scissors and tape — and it's just a terrible mess. I only keep it for sentimental reasons now because I want to laugh at myself every time I look at it!

CHAPTER TWENTY-THREE

A powerful technique for writing sales letters that can make you millions of dollars.

Always write more sales copy than you actually need, and then start cutting. That way you're able to boil it down and only use the hardest-hitting sales copy. **One thing you have to learn,** that you have to internalize, **is the fact that writing and rewriting should be looked at as two entirely separate things.** A lot of people don't do that: they write and edit at the same time. I think this is one of the fundamental things that screws people up when they try to write something, because they're too critical. The time you're actually putting that copy on a computer screen or jotting it down on legal pads is a time for getting your ideas out there. It's not the time to be critical. You just want to get as much on the page as you can, as fast as you can.

What I love to do when I'm writing is get up real early every morning. I make my first pot of coffee really strong. It's definitely one of the last legal drugs in the world, and I'm definitely addicted! When I wake up in the morning I'll be half asleep, and I'll drink half a pot of real strong black coffee and just start writing. I won't even worry about whether I'm spelling correctly. I won't try to break my paragraphs. I won't even look at the screen half of the time, except to make sure I didn't hit the all-caps button by accident or something like that. I'll write while I'm high on coffee; then, later in the afternoon, when I'm really tired and all I can do is shuffle papers because my brain is dead, I'll go through and painstakingly break all the paragraphs up, handle the misspelling and all that crap, and try and make something legible out of the mess I created in the morning. **I have to tell you, that's one of the best techniques that I've ever learned: don't try and do it in one step. Do it in two.**

Another thing: as my friend and colleague Don Bice has pointed out to me, the way to get a lot of good ideas is to get a lot of good ideas! **The more ideas you come up with, the** *better* **ideas you'll come up with.** That whole concept transfers directly to writing sales copy. **The way to get great copy is to come up with lots of copy, and then take those little gems you've written and tell yourself, "I'm only going to keep half of what I've got here."** You discipline yourself, and promise yourself you'll cut half of what you just wrote. Now, you're not under pressure to try and come up with something good; you're just under pressure to try to jam it all out. **Later on you can start the mundane task of editing. That's when you polish your work.** Many's the time when I've looked at my copy and said, "Whoa! This intro is the perfect *ending*. I could use it at the end." Maybe I'll find the second paragraph is a better opening. <u>When you're editing and rewriting, you find stuff that's impossible to find when you're "in the moment."</u> If editing isn't your forte, or it's not the best use of your time, you can always hire an editor pretty easily.

You have to **get yourself out of the mindset of thinking, when you sit down to write, that it's got to come out in the first draft exactly the way it'll look in the last draft.** This just gets in your way. My colleague Jeff Gardner tells me he used to have problems with this. He'd start with the pre-head and try and get that perfect. Then he'd go on to the headline and try and get that perfect, and then treat the sub-heads the same. Not only did he want everything to sound perfect, but he also wanted perfect formatting. Well, he realized very quickly that's the worst way ever to write a sales letter because that's when you're talking about taking two or three months to complete it. That's simply not the way it's done. Your brain doesn't work like that. <u>You</u> <u>can't</u> <u>be</u> <u>creative</u> <u>and</u> <u>judgmental</u> <u>at</u> <u>the</u> <u>exact</u> <u>same</u> <u>time</u>. Try it, and your brain starts to shut down.

What you need to do is completely switch off the judge in your head, sit down, and rush through 10, 15, or 20 pages. **Just start writing, and don't judge at all or edit at all at that point.** Later on in the day, or even maybe a day or two later go back through and edit. When you do that, you'll find that you don't necessarily have to do a whole lot of editing; the writing's often better than the judge in your head thought! **You can end up with some pretty good copy if you didn't judge yourself and stop to edit everything while you're writing it.** <u>And</u> <u>don't</u> <u>over-edit,</u> <u>either</u>; at some point you've got to stop agonizing and send those babies out into the world. **In the effort to make it perfect, you can kill what's special about your copy by homogenizing it or making it look too polished.**

Now, this isn't a process you're going to master right away; it'll take time. There's a learning curve you have to go through, so you can't be afraid of enduring a little bit of pain and confusion in the beginning. I have a good friend who's an entrepreneur. I gave him some marketing tapes and he complained to me that he had to stop listening because he was just getting so confused. To me, confusion is just part of it. Confusion isn't a bad thing. **This is a skill that you can develop and master, and it's worth the effort because learning how to become a good copywriter will pay off in so many dividends it's incredible.**

CHAPTER TWENTY-FOUR

The major mistake most business people are making... and how you can avoid it.

Most business owners don't have a systematic strategy for marketing, and **they don't track what's working and what isn't.** That can be a huge mistake because you've all heard the old saying that goes, *"About half my advertising is working, and about half of it isn't — but I don't know which half is which."* I hate to admit it, but sometimes that's true with me. If I'm tracking some advertising from, say, three or four magazines where we're running inquiry ads and the program is going well, sometimes I'll just put ads in ten more magazines and stop the tracking process. That's a mistake, but if things are going well it's not so important to track. It's important, though, especially when you're first starting.

People do everything they can think of to get business, and some of it's working and some of it's not. **Most people never think about the processes and methods for (1) attracting new customers, (2) selling them for the largest profit, and (3) reselling them as often as possible for the maximum profits.** All their marketing activities are hit and miss. That's true with so many of us, beginners particularly. They never quantify what's working the best. Without this quantification they can never combine the best methods into any kind of reliable, automatic marketing system.

That's what we're all searching for — to get something working well, and then turn it into an automatic cash-flow moneymaking system. **It all relates to optimizing profits from every new buyer or new potential buyer we get.** Remember what I've said previously: that your first contact with some responder is just that. You've heard from a responder. Then, once they buy (if they take it that far) they become a buyer. **The ultimate goal is to turn buyers into customers we can to sell again and again.** If you have customers, you have the backbone of a great business, and the potential to make millions of dollars. We strive to get these responders and turn them into buyers, and then turn the buyers into customers who will stay with us year after year.

To do this, we must continue to sell our customers products similar to the ones they first responded to — over and over again. I've said this already many times, but it bears repeating. **You should be in contact with these people at least 10 or 12 times a year.** Don't let them get cold. Whatever they want to buy, they're going to buy. If they don't buy it from you, they'll buy it from your competitors. That's why it's so important to turn those responders into buyers, and buyers into customers, and then to treat them like kings and queens. Service them well, and keep giving them what they want. If you do that, you can get rich in Direct-Response Marketing.

Let me demonstrate, through a personal example, how this principle can be worth a fortune to you. At our company, we're constantly running different promotions, so we're always testing different things. A lot of our tests are small, and the reason why we test things on a small basis is because we're trying not to be fools. If you only spend a few thousand dollars on a test and it fails, then you only lose a few thousand dollars instead of ten times that much. Sometimes promotions work so well that you lose sight of some of the other things you're testing. Recently, that's exactly what happened to us. In the midst of some really great promotions that were working well for us we forgot about this one small test that we did. It was actually a joint venture with Don Bice. We weren't watching the numbers on it very carefully, and all of a sudden we realized that the numbers on the front end weren't too good. I remember noticing that, and then I lost interest; I lost track of the whole promotion and got sidetracked. Then one of the staff came up to me and said, "Hey, T.J., this promotion worked a little better than you thought." He showed me that the back-end conversion was 36 percent. I freaked out; I just couldn't believe it. **With the information that we got from that test, we're going to roll it out with a lot of different things, since it's based on a concept that can be stamped out and used for God knows how many promotions.** We might end up finding 50 ways to use this concept we're going to steal from Don! Of course, he gave us permission to steal it.

The point is, unless you're watching the numbers very carefully, you can miss things. **You have to watch everything as carefully as you can, even those small tests, because you need to be able to take the winning themes and concepts and use them again and again.** As long as you do it carefully, you can make millions. This works even if your company isn't huge. Don't assume, like some marketers do, that testing is only for the big guys who can afford it. Even if your client list is relatively small, you can test to your best customers in order to determine whether or not what you're testing has the proper appeal. If it doesn't work with those people, then you know it's not going to work with the others. Admittedly, some of the tests are subtle, but expensive. If you have a full-page ad in a magazine, for example, you can leave the whole ad the same but change the headline and see your sales more than double. That's an expensive test, but it's the kind of testing you really want to zero in on. **Often, people get so close to hitting it big, and they don't realize it because they're missing just a few little pieces of the puzzle.**

CHAPTER TWENTY-FIVE

The power of pressure.

In the midnight hour, when the deadlines are closing in, you're forced to make decisions. **The walls of indecision begin breaking down, and the answers that were once very muddy become clear.** I think this is a very powerful principle because human nature is that we're all procrastinators. We love to push decisions off as long as possible. We like to wait for the final hour to do things. We all tend to procrastinate. We wait and we wait until stuff absolutely has to be done before we do it — whatever it is.

In the business world, it's mostly the same thing. **Unless you have a tight deadline, you simply keep putting things off until later.** You wait until tomorrow, and tomorrow becomes the next day, and pretty soon nothing gets done. Without deadlines, decisions that need to be made just keep getting pushed back more and more, and things never get done. One of the nice things about deadlines is that they don't have to be set by someone else. In fact, **one of the best things you can do for yourself is to set your own self-imposed deadlines.** Just make a note on your calendar that by X date you're going to have it accomplished. Even though there's no one to push you to it, just writing things down can actually help you accomplish your goals.

If your goal is to write a sales letter, set a time that you have to be finished by. Maybe you have to get a website up on the Internet; set yourself a deadline. **You might even try telling people about your deadline.** Sometimes if you set your own deadline, it's easy to break it — but if you tell someone else about it or write it down somewhere where someone else can see, then you have someone else to hold you to that deadline.

One of the best ways to set deadlines is to make a decision that forces the deadline upon you. It makes something else have to happen so you have to meet that deadline. For example, if you're writing an offer, maybe you have a pre-publication sale where you're selling your product before it's even created. In your sales material, you could tell the customers that your product will be finished in two or three weeks, or four to six weeks, or whatever your self-imposed deadline is. **By putting it down in black-and-white in your pre-publication offer, you're forced to finish the product before the deadline.** You have this product that needs to be created, and you have people who have given you money to create that product on a pre-publication basis, so **now you have to produce.**

The same thing is true for other deadlines. You could give your printer a deadline that says that next Tuesday you're going to have the sales material to them, so they can print your offer and you can get it in the mail. Maybe you have a mailing house, and you have them lined up so that on a particular date they're expecting your printer to deliver the materials to get your promotion out the door. **Having someone else waiting on you to give them material by a certain deadline spurs you into action and forces you to complete the project.** In the midnight hour, when the deadlines are closing in, you're forced to make decisions. **That's the positive power of pressure. As soon as you're finished with this particular topic, I challenge you set your first deadline.** Put this down for a little while and set a deadline. It doesn't matter if it relates to your website or a mailing you've been thinking about, or a product you've been considering. Put this down, get out a piece of paper, write down something you want to do, and a date you want to have it done by. Then share it with a few people, and you can start to move forward.

Until you actually set goals and deadlines for yourself, you're just going to keep putting things off. Like I said, we're all procrastinators. It's a human flaw. It's something we all struggle with, so don't think you're alone. But you have to overcome human nature; you have to set those deadlines to be able to move forward and start making more money.

Confusion tends to fall away the closer you're to the deadline. This is because so many of us wait to get things done because they want to have everything figured out first. They want all the answers to be clear, so they're not going to set a goal. They want to be comfortable first — because they're afraid that maybe they're not going to be able to pull it off. But most projects don't work that way. Personally, I like to just set the goal for the project and get going.

Chris Lakey was recently doing a promotional tape, and Jeff Gardner was helping us with it. At the end Chris and Jeff gave their contact information for any customers who were interested. Chris said, "Go to my website, and there's a special button there for you guys listening to this recording. Click that special button, and I have a special offer for just nine of you." After the call was over I said to Chris, "Hey, Chris, that was really smart. What's that button on your website all about?" Chris said, "Oh, I don't know yet!"

I love that, because now he has all these people who are going to listen to that CD and, by God, he's forced to get that button on his site. Now he's going to have to put a button up there that says "For Beta Testers Only." That was the group we were talking to. Then he's going to have to figure out where they go when they hit that button because, by God, there better be something up there, or else he'll lose money. But you know what? Chris did exactly right. **I think a deadline is absolutely imperative for any project you're wanting to accomplish.** It gives you a lot of time to work on something. The real problem solving comes in the sub-conscious mind, on a continuing basis. So, when you define a problem and you say to yourself, "I need to do that by this or that date," your mind begins to work on it. All those days that are going between when you're putting it off and saying, "I'm going to do it tomorrow," what's really happening is that at some level, your mind is working on the problem. Then, when you get close enough to the deadline, you have to deliver. **Your mind gathers all those thoughts it's been considering below your consciousness, organizes them better than you would do consciously, and makes material available to you to solve your problem.** It really works that way, and that's why deadlines are so very important.

Billy Barnes was the songwriter musician who wrote all the music for the *Carol Burnett Show*, as well as *Laugh In* and the specialty material for a lot of celebrities, and he said once that he wished he had a dollar for every time he was still writing notes in the back of the cab on his sheet music on the way to CBS for rehearsals. He said maybe he had six weeks to do it and he thought about it for six weeks, but it all came to pass because he had a deadline and he had to stand and deliver. We need to do that in our own lives. I know I have to because, without that, there's always a little more time to think about it and a way to change it just a little more. I think, "Tomorrow I'll look at it again," and <u>without a deadline it just keeps getting worked on occasionally and never completed</u>.

Meeting financial obligations creates even more pressure than self-imposed deadlines. For example, if you have infrastructure and you know that every month you have to pay out a set amount for the infrastructure, boy, you have some real pressure to make at least that amount of money so your business can continue! I know that in the past in my business, I've purchased things — whether it's a home or a car or something like that — and I say, "Okay, my business has to do this amount of money every single month so I can pay for this." When I look at the financial statements and see that the business is tapering off, or I need to have a real big burst, then I get out there and I write a letter and make a great offer. **I put all my time and effort into it because I know I've got to meet that financial obligation.**

I know a famous self-made millionaire, and I asked him once, *"Hey, if you had to boil it down to one sentence, what is the secret of your success?"* He said, *"I love making money, and I'm married to a woman who absolutely loves to spend money!"* Seriously, those same financial pressures that can cause some people to jump off buildings, or slit their wrists, or drink and drug themselves to death, causes other people to accomplish great things. **It all comes down to how we channel our energy.** Consider the old metaphor of a ship: the same wind can carry a ship, or make it impossible for a ship to pass. It's in how you set the sails. Some of the times over the years that I've been the least motivated have been when business was too good. In looking back at it now, **the best breakthroughs always occur when business sucks.** When business is getting bad, that's when I go to work; when business gets good, I never put as much into it.

I think **you have to identify what motivates you** because different things motivate different people. Financial obligation doesn't motivate some folks — it paralyzes them. If you point out to these people the financial obligations they're under and how large they are, those people may end up paralyzed with fear. You've got to know if that's how you're going to react. With the same people you may be able to point out, "But look, you can solve this problem by creating this or that." The creative part excites them and motivates them to solve the problem.

One story I always love is about marketer Gary Halbert, who offered a marketing seminar quite a few years ago and had a lot of big name marketers coming in to speak. The first day they did all the speaking in the morning, and he invited everybody up to his room over the lunchtime. The marketers all thought, "Hey, we're going to get a free lunch and have some time to relax!" But Gary got everybody up there and said, "Okay, now we have to figure out something to sell these people! No one is eating any lunch. We'll be brainstorming the next product to sell these people we have here." Talk about pressure! But that's what they did over lunch. <u>They came up with that next product right there, and then they went down and sold it</u>.

There's nothing like a pre-publication sale to motivate me because I'm committed to the customers. I don't want the customers being too upset. If a few customers are ticked off I don't lose sleep over it, but when I have a whole group of customers who are upset, that bothers me. When I think about 300 customers who are expecting their package, and they've all have sent us money and all 300 of them are sitting there waiting for their package and they're all getting more ticked off every single day that that package doesn't come in the mail — well, that bothers me. All of a sudden I become the most motivated person in the world. **For most marketers, that's the absolute requirement to getting things done on time. We all want to serve our customers.** The last thing we want is a group of customers who are all angry with us.

CHAPTER TWENTY-SIX

Getting back to the basics.

Barry Gordy, the founder of Motown records, was once quoted as saying, "It's all about supply and demand." And speaking of supply and demand, that's what the concept of take-away selling is based on. **You have to do everything possible to increase the perception of the demand, and to increase the perception of a decrease in supply.** There are many different ways you can do this. I'll talk about a few in this section.

The power of supply and demand is quite simple. Number one, you have to increase the demand for something. You know the rumors you hear about these natural-born sales people who can sell refrigerators to Eskimos? I think that's a bunch of crap. I don't think anybody can sell refrigerators to people who live in igloos. **There has to be some demand for what you have already; you can't just manufacture demand.** You have to be in a market that desires the benefits that your company sells.

It all starts with a good, qualified prospect. If you have a good, qualified prospect who already has a demand for the kind of benefits your product or service provides, then you can do things to crank that volume wide open. Some of those things you can do by creating more benefits in your sales copy. You can give them more reasons why it'll serve them to buy from you. You can increase the excitement. Throw in a little hype. Throw in a little sizzle! Make it sound exciting! You can try to make them visualize owning it. I like what Gene

Schwartz said, when he was talking about good mail order advertising copy: that it's like a window on Main Street, where the customers are walking along and looking in those windows. **Your copy has to make people look through the window and see themselves with the item you're trying to sell them.** This is more important if you're doing it over the Internet or mail order rather than with a retail business.

The second part of the formula is the real key here: **you have to do something to decrease the perception of the supply.** Notice that I chose those words very carefully. You don't have to decrease the supply, but you have to decrease the *perception* of it. Some of the ways I've seen some marketers do it over the years border on the illegal. I won't talk about those. What you can do, quite legally, is limit the number of available positions. You set very tight deadlines that people have to respond to. Then, give them a strong reason why you're having this special sale. Try to make it as believable as possible. The more believable you can make all these things, the more you're able to make people want it really badly, which is part of increasing the demand. You have to make 'em hot for it.

Speaking of **supply and demand,** my friend Russ Von Hoelscher had a girlfriend several years back who was big into antiques. Once she was looking for some lamps, so they went into this store in Kensington, in San Diego, where there are 10 or 12 antique dealers in a two-block area. Russ told me that one lamp was priced at $100 and was really good looking, but it really wasn't an antique. It was an old lamp and very ornate and it was very nice. Then there was this ugly thing that was $600 that *was* a real antique. He said, "For gosh sakes, this $100 lamp is many times nicer than this $600 lamp." She said, "Yeah, but this other one is from France and it's an antique." So she bought both of them. Russ noticed later that the antique went into a storage area, while the good-looking lamp got put up in the living room and used every day. That's a perfect example, I think, of how if something's rare , people will buy it, even if it's God-awful ugly.

Another example involves the PT Cruiser — that weird-looking car that Daimler-Chrysler came out with a few years ago. Actually, I kind of like them. They're pretty neat, but they were in rare supply. They showed a prototype to the magazines and to the car-buying public and then said, "But we can't supply them for several months." I had a friend in St. Paul, Minnesota who put in his order for one of them but didn't get it for almost six months. People all over the country all of a sudden wanted these cars. They were hard to get, which made them even more enticing. It's a perfect example of supply and demand. When we're selling stuff, we have to say things like, "We're only accepting 100 members," or, "I'm only going to work with 100 dealers," or "I only published 1,000 of these manuals; first come, first served, etc., etc.," because **people like what's in limited supply. When the supply is limited, the demand goes sky high.**

Look at the toy industry. They're famous for creating supply and demand. Look what they did with Cabbage Patch Dolls a number of years ago. Remember how people fought over those things because they were in limited quantity? They did the same thing when some of the PlayStation games came out for Christmas. There was only going to be a small number of them and people fought to get them. The toy industry has made supply and demand a fine art because they have money behind them to make it widely known that certain items are in limited supply. They pre-sell you, and then tell you there aren't many of what they've pre-sold you on available. For those of us with smaller budgets than Mattel or Sony it's a little more difficult to do, but it still works, whether you're selling information or toys or almost anything.

It's very basic economics. When those scarce toys came out, you could go onto eBay, for example, and find people selling Cabbage Patch dolls or Tickle Me Elmos or PlayStation game consoles for thousands of dollars more than their manufacturers sold them for, just because the demand was high but the supply was incredibly low. That's the great thing about limiting the supply of your product. Whenever you limit the supply and say, "Okay, there are only 50 or 100 of these and no more," **you can automatically ask for a higher amount of money if the demand is there.** You may say in your letter that the supply is limited, but it may just be limited to as many as you want to make and sell.

Here's an interesting example from my friend Jeff Gardner. He really likes this idea about limiting things and providing scarcity, so he's putting together an audio CD package of his innermost secrets on a particular topic — but there's a catch. He wants to have eight cassette tapes in the set, and doesn't just want to just sell these for $50 or $100; he wants to sell them for $1,000. How can he do that? Well, he thought, "I really need to make this a scarce offer," so he created this story about how they're his innermost secrets, and they're never going to be revealed again. He's only going to create 100 sets of these eight audio CD's. After the 100 have been duplicated, he's going to take a hammer to those masters and crush them all, so that there could never be a number 101 or 102 in the edition. The 100 that are in existence will be it. That's the story. That's actually in testing right now, and if Jeff has any luck, it'll work. If he sells the 100 at $1,000 each that'll be $100,000, so he doesn't mind crushing those masters. The information is still in Jeff's head so, if he decides to on put similar information on different CD's, videotapes or a book later on, he could certainly do that.

In the magic business, a publisher by the name of Robert Harbin did that a number of years ago. He wrote a book and said he was going to print 500 or 1,000 copies, and at the end he would destroy the plates. It was a good book — and that book's now worth anywhere up to $1,000, depending on how badly someone wants it as a collector's item. **He created that scarcity.**

Recently a friend of mine wrote a book and went to a society meeting in England. He wrote this publication as he was giving a lecture, and he was going to offer this book for sale at the close of the lecture. He told the society they could keep 100 percent of the profits for the organization and he would give them these copies. They said, "Well, how much should we sell it for?" He said, "Probably $50, because all of the money is going to your organization." They said, "Oh, $50. We could never ask people $50 for this. We'll ask them for $10." So they sold the books for $10, and they only sold a handful. A short time later someone went on eBay and wanted a copy, and it was bid up to $650. His phone started ringing off the wall with people calling to buy the book. Everyone wanted the book now because it was $650. They wanted to get their hands on it, but when it was $10, they weren't interested!

The concept operating here is that if everyone can have it, then nobody wants it. Write that down and think about it. **You have to build this in as part of your creative offers to really sell them.** Somehow, there has to be scarcity involved. Consider the way Jeff Gardner's planning to take a hammer and smash his master CD's — he's increasing the demand, and making it sound exciting in the process. People can visualize it. He is going to go outside in his driveway and he's going to grab a hammer out of his toolbox and he's going to smash those CD's! It sounds interesting, doesn't it?

If you don't want to go that far, **a limited edition is always a good idea, especially if it's signed and numbered.** You're selling exclusivity. People like to think they have something that not everyone else has. You can add value that way even if you offer it in two levels. You can have the regular edition at whatever price, and then you have the signed, limited edition for an additional price. It's amazing how **many people will choose that deluxe version of the same product because they see it as having more value.** It's more exclusive, and fewer people will have that edition.

There's a marketing consultant who's very successful and charges $800 to $1,000 an hour for telephone consulting. He says that even years ago when he first got started, even though he was practically starving to death and barely getting by, he understood this concept. From Day One, he was always hard to get a hold of. When a new client would call him with a job they needed done right away, his schedule was always too busy and he could never get to it for another two or three weeks — even though he needed the work desperately and had nothing but time on his hands. **He created the perception that his time was in short supply. I want you to think long and hard about this: perception is reality.**

Your biggest job as a marketer is to overcome the skepticism of your customers, and make them perceive that reality is the way you present it. Basically, people want to believe. **So you try to address and overcome their skepticism.** If you can do a good enough job at that, you're going to make a lot of money. There are a lot of different ways to do that, depending upon the medium you're working in. In written copy, you have to have a headline that grabs them. You can also create exclusivity by establishing criteria. For instance, let's say you're selling something like auto responders. You might have a list of eight must-have criteria to evaluate an auto responder. Guess what? Yours is the only one that meets all eight, so you eliminate the competition. **You can also get their emotions involved.** When you're limiting the availability, you're dealing with emotions just as you are with perception. That's one vital and important technique in any marketing arsenal.

Recently, Chris Lakey came up with a new promotion for

our company where we're giving away websites, absolutely free. There's an entry fee people have to pay, but once they pay it, they get these websites absolutely free. Chris tells people right away that if they had to go to a developer for sites, these web sites would sell for several thousand dollars — just for development alone. Forget the hosting charges, and forget the copywriting. He goes on and on and on about that — page after page of explaining why these websites really are worth $3,000 or $4,000 — and then he shows people why we can afford to give them away free. He makes a very clear and compelling case. He uses about 20 pages of copy to do this. **By convincing people that it's worth this amount of money and then showing them exactly why he's able to do it, Chris has created an offer that people are going to go wild over.**

The thing that excites me about the whole thing is that **we don't think it's ever been done before** — that is, where you're actually giving them a website before they've even said that they wanted it. But here's an important point: if Chris hadn't taken the time to go through 20-odd pages explaining it all to them, if he'd tried to just do it in a small letter, they would have looked at it and said, "This is crap," and would have thrown it away and stomped on it. They'd have bad feelings toward us because they'd think we're trying to scam them. **This just goes to show that you have to build up a strong case.**

CHAPTER TWENTY-SEVEN

Just Do It!

Here is a tip from my Ruthless Marketing Manual: *"Action has its own wisdom. You learn in a very deep way by going through the pain of solving daily problems, working on new promotions to bring in more money, setting bigger goals and biting off more than you can chew."* This tip is so important. We've touched on this before, but I really want to hammer it home, because a lot of people just never get started. Why? Because if they don't get started, they don't have to worry. A lot of people in this business worry about every little thing. They worry about competition. They worry about having to maintain an office: dealing with a computer, having employees to deal with, overhead. **They worry so much about all this crap they never get started.** Most people are so busy overanalyzing and planning that they never start their business at all — and if you don't start your business, you can't make even a dollar. Heck, you can't make a *penny* if you don't get started.

I think it's very important to stop overanalyzing and planning, and just get busy doing something. Even if you do something wrong, at least you're taking action. Some people say it's okay to fail as long as you fail forward; **in other words, move in a positive direction.** I realize it's far too easy to fall into the trap of overanalyzing and planning too much. Let's say, for example, that you're brand new to business and you want to start up a new company. You go to the library or bookstore and look for books on starting a new business. That may sound like you're moving in the right direction, but personally I think it's one of the worst things you can do. I'm not saying that books are bad, but if you pick up these books you'll find that most of them take you through 200-300 pages or more just on starting a new business. Now, in many cases they're going to go on about taxes, and talking to the county clerk, and employees and tons of stuff you may never have to worry about. What those books will say is that you'd better read every page and know exactly how to set up your business before you try because if you do it the wrong way, all sorts of bad things are going to happen to you.

Ignore all of that stuff. **Find out what you need to do to start your business, and get started.** My friend Jeff Gardner tells this story: many years ago, when he first got involved in mail-order business, setting up his own business seemed like a daunting task. Every time he'd go back to the library or bookstore, there would be more and more books on setting up and starting your business. So, every year in January he'd write on his goal list, "This year I'm setting up my own business." Then the whole year would go by and he wouldn't get it done. January would come and he'd tell himself again, "This year I'm setting up my own business." Then the *next* year would go by. Finally Jeff got tired of it and said to himself, "Look, I'm going to find out what it takes." He called up the county clerk and said, "I'm going to start up a business. I know it's a long process, and I know it's going to take me a lot of time and paperwork to do it — but what do I need to do?" She said, "Send me $15. Then go to the bank and set up a checking account, and boom, you're in business!" **In about 30 minutes Jeff had set up the business he'd believed would take mounds of paperwork and massive effort to accomplish.**

People tend to make things way too complicated. All of these books on getting started in your own business are just so much crap. They focus on a bunch of meaningless nonsense. But you can't sell too many books if you can put it all on a 3 x 5 card, which you can easily do. The fact is, most of the "experts" out there writing these books have never started a business themselves! If they've been in business, they've always worked as a middle manager for some large corporation. **Here's the secret: focus on yourself and profits.** Just think about making money. Throw all your receipts in a shoebox, then take your receipts to the accountant at the end of the year and say, "Look, here's everything. I'm completely confused. I don't do math. I don't do numbers. I don't do taxes. You figure it out. If you need any help, don't call me, because I'm confused." It's pretty much as simple as that.

What I've found over the years is that a lot of the things you build up in your mind never end up causing problems. **Getting started, marketing, finding or creating products — it's never as difficult as your mind builds it up to be.** What you need to do is forget all that fear and just start taking action. I know a lot of writers who don't much worry about what they're writing on a day-to-day basis. They know that to create a book or a product, they just need to get started. They don't worry about the quality as they're writing. They don't judge it as they go; **they just sit down and they take action.** They may write for an hour. Then the next day, when they look at the pages they wrote the previous day they may say, "That's garbage and I'm going to throw it away." But what they've done is taken action — and they've gotten in the habit of taking action. So, every single day, day after day, they write. Every single day, day after day, **the most successful marketers set aside time to market their products or to build their business. That's really the key: taking action.** Again, it's a simple idea, but it's the most powerful one out there because every single marketing technique that I'm giving you is absolutely useless if you don't take action.

My friend Russ von Hoelscher has said many times over

the years that **the one thing that robs people of success more than anything else is simply not getting started.** Some people plan until Kingdom come. They're forever planning, forever thinking, forever trying to figure out a way they should start. **Just do it! Get started now!** Even if you make some mistakes, even if things aren't perfect, even if you don't know everything. You'll never stop making mistakes no matter how good you are, and you'll never know everything you think you should know. But just getting started puts you in the game, and that's where the action is. That's where you can do something meaningful.

How to do something always comes last. What comes first is the courage to do it. Think of a battle, where you might have a platoon that's in serious danger and one guy says, "I have to protect everybody." What does he do? He may just jump up and start firing away blindly, creating a diversion. That decision was backed by whatever was available to him. Fortunately it's much easier with marketing, **but the decision, the determination to get started, is what's important. Then you figure out how.**

I know a lot of people are saying, "But I don't have any courage. I'm not sure if I can run straight forward like that." Well, courage doesn't mean you don't have any fear. Courage isn't the absence of fear. **Courage means taking action even when fear is present.** Even when you're not sure what's going on, or you're confused, or you're thinking, "Hey, I may fail." Some people actually have a fear of success; they think, "I may do really well, and then I'll have all these other problems to deal with." Either way, courage is putting those fears aside, working through them, and taking action in spite of them. You're never going to come to a point where you're not tentative about something, whether it's in your business or your personal life. But to really get to your goals and achieve success, whether it's in marketing or business or anything else, **you need to push those fears aside, buck**

---

up, and have that courage to move ahead and take action, even if you might fail — even if you stumble and fall.

Jeff Gardner once told me that one of the best things he was ever told was that he was going to fail. Well, that's the way it is; it's an absolute. You're going to continue to fail. Your entire life, you're going to fail and fail again. You may say, "Oh, that's a horrible thing to say!" But it's reality. **You have to be realistic in business and understand that one failure isn't the end. You're not *always* going to fail.** But if you realize that you're going to stumble and fall every so often, then you can live through it. You're not tentative. You're not curled up in the fetal position on your bed, afraid to go out in the world. If you realize you're going to stumble and fall and skin your knee, then you're better able to get right back up and keep moving forward when it happens. **It's the people who are able to get back up and walk through failure who are successful.**

If you read the biography of any self-made millionaire or billionaire, you'll see that they never woke up one day and said, "Okay, I'm going to be rich," and moved right to riches and never had a problem. In many cases, these people acquired and lost their wealth many times over. Some of them went bankrupt. They were in the poorhouse — and they came back again and again. You have to have that attitude. If you don't, you'll never reach your ultimate goals.

Often, confidence comes from experience. Now, that's bad for the person who has no experience, but the point is that, oftentimes, you see these very successful entrepreneurs and they're practically strutting. You can tell that they're brimming over with confidence. Some of them are cockier than hell, but they have reason to be. A lot of these very successful entrepreneurs exhibit this spirit. There's a look of confidence in their eyes. You start thinking, "Maybe they were somehow born with that confidence." That was one of the things that really bothered me because, in the beginning, I didn't have any confidence. I was filled with all kinds of fears and insecurities. I saw these people who were very successful, and I thought, "Man, I can't be like that."

These people showed no fear. I used to be intimidated just being in the same room with them. What I've found since then is that some of them are just faking it. They might be scared to death, but they're acting like they're confident. Even so, **many of them are people who've built their confidence over a period of time.** They've experienced their failures and they've learned from their mistakes. They keep improving their game. They keep getting stronger and they keep getting better. They learn more and, as they learn more, they're able to do more.

This ability comes from increased experience, but it also comes from the attitude that, *"Hey, if he can do that, so can I!"* I think we need to adopt that attitude more and more. Don't look at speakers, writers, marketers, or anyone else as having special gifts you could never match. **If you really want to do what they do, and you have the desire, then the correct attitude is, "There's no reason I can't do it."**

CHAPTER TWENTY-EIGHT

Be ruthless and restless.

A famous marketing expert has coined a sentence he calls his "entrepreneurial prayer." It goes like this: "Dear lord, please keep me restless and ruthless." Now, what the heck does he mean by that? I think this is what he means: **complacency is one of the chief enemies of greater success.** Once you start enjoying success, it's easy to get yourself in a rut and adopt a "Hey, I'm doing okay, things aren't too bad, everything is copacetic" attitude. But, **when you're restless (and I think restlessness is related to desire) then you keep wanting more, more, more.** Not just more money, but more challenges, more creativity, more victories in the battlefield of life and in the battlefield of business. This really keeps you moving forward. In business, we're either moving forward or we're going backwards. I really believe that. If you're standing still, you're really going backward, because the world just keeps on spinning. I think we have to be restless. We have to want more for ourselves and our families: more fulfillment, not just money, although that's part of it. **We're expanding, or we're contracting.** It's much better to be expanding, to be reaching forward, searching for that next big breakthrough. It's just slightly out of reach, but if we keep going forward, we can get to it.

Now as far as "Lord keep me ruthless" goes, **we must remain stealthy and search for new methods and strategies to beat the competition and achieve even greater success.** If you're going to knock out your competition, you need to know exactly what the competition is doing. That means you want to be on their mailing lists. That means you want to be reading their ads. That means you want to be visiting their websites. You want to know as much about their business as you possibly can, in order to see what they're doing right and what they're doing wrong. **It's much easier to be successful with a project that you steal from someone else than with a project you create from scratch!**

Now, when I say "steal," **I don't mean you should take their idea word for word, or take their service or their product and sell it just the way it is.** I'm talking about learning what they're doing right and what they're doing wrong, and creating a better product than they have. Then market the hell out of it. I think that's what really keeps us ruthless — constantly looking for things that we can enhance, embellish, and then market better by writing better copy and bringing it to the public. Speaking of ruthlessness, I don't feel that we're being ruthless in the sense that a lot of people think we are. You can describe the worst kind of characters on this planet as being ruthless. In our business, I think **ruthlessness is more of a hunger.** I see it as just being hungry for your customer's money and being willing to do whatever you have to legally, morally, and ethically to get that money. That's ruthless to me.

I also think that **the terms "restless" and "ruthless" are well combined.** It's an energy you're committed to; you're driven to make all the money you can. It gets back to what I was talking about in a previous section about craftiness. You can enjoy designing another play that pulls out even more money from another select group of customers. **You have to set higher goals.** One of my favorite quotes is, *"The only sin in life is having a low aim."* **Most people just don't reach for enough,** I think. That's the reason they're not restless. I see people in this world who are totally content. I don't understand those people, because I've *never* been

---

totally contented. I've always wanted more. I believe this is something I share with most successful entrepreneurs — there's always a certain amount of discontent in their natures. They become successful because they're so discontented and so restless. If you decide to start a business but you're content just the way you are with your present job, your chances for success are minimal because **it's the restlessness and the discontent that will drive you to do more and better things.**

So let me put it this way: **if you're happy with the way things are now, then the business world may not be for you.** You may have had that seed of enterprise implanted by the media or by your family, but if you're someone who just wants to be content, you might not get very far on your own. **Every entrepreneur, I've discovered, is restless at some level. They don't want contentment.** They're so constantly after bigger and better things that you'd think that these people have attention deficit disorder because **they jump from one opportunity and one challenge to another.** They just continue to go and go and go. If that's not your personality, then you might need to look somewhere else. But if that *is* your personality, you're in exactly the right spot because you have all the personality traits to be a great entrepreneur. This point goes with what I've talked about before, about not having to have everything planned out all the time. Your restlessness in and of itself creates the opportunities. There's a quote that says that talent always rises to the top. Everybody can agree with that. They see other people as being very talented, and they know that people with a certain degree of talent always seem to rise above everyone else. But there's another quote that fewer people have heard about. **It says that many times, it's your desire that creates your talent.** I love that distinction because if you want something bad enough, you'll develop the talent it takes to get it.

CHAPTER TWENTY-NINE

Marketing wisdom from a master showman.

Johnny Carson once said, "It's not the audience who has the power, it's me. It's my talent and ability to know how to keep giving them what they want. I'm in control; not them." This quote comes from an interview he did with *Playboy* magazine. Here's another quote from my Ruthless Marketing Program: *"Yes, the market comes first, of course, but it's the marketer's ability to read that market and discover the most powerful and profitable ways to serve that market that counts the most."* In other words, he's is saying the **control is in *our* hands, not theirs.** This gives you a lot of power.

This is an extremely important point because, as a marketer, you have to be in total control of your situation. Yes, we're here to serve our customers and to some degree we consider them our bosses — but using an analogy, we have to be like that secretary who can get her way with the boss just by knowing how to play him like a fiddle. **We have to be that person who knows just the right buttons to push in order to make people respond the way he wants them to.** While Johnny Carson served a different market than most of us, the concept is still the same. As he said, "It's my talent and ability to know how to keep giving them what they want," that made him so successful. He said, "I'm in control, not them." **You have to be in control, constantly.** Your goal should always be to study your market, to know your market and be able to respond by giving your customers the kinds of products and services they desperately want. The more they want them, the more money you can make from them.

There's a saying that goes something like this: *"If you fill a need you can make a living, but if you fill a want, you can get rich."* **Your ticket to big fortune is having the talent and ability to know how to keep giving your customers exactly what they want.** If you want to make biggest profits possible, you have to follow Johnny Carson's principle. You have to begin with the understanding that the buck starts and stops with you. You're in total control of the situation and maybe that's scary to you. But don't let it be because it actually gives you the kind of power that few people ever get the chance to experience. **It's the power of being able to push people's buttons, of knowing how to make customer do exactly what you want them to do — which is to send you their money.** With that power, with that control and the responsibility of being in control of the situation and knowing what your customers want, you have the potential to accumulate great wealth.

The late, great Ray Krock, the man who took McDonald's into the stratosphere, once said *"Selling is letting the customer have it our way."* I like that because, although there are all sorts of situations when the market dictates to us, in most circumstances *we're* the ones in charge. Where the ones who make the customers want it the way we want to give it to them. We're the ones who have control over the way we communicate our different sales and marketing messages. We're the ones who can do things to help build that bond between us and the customers. If you ever get to feeling that the market dictates you, or that the market has total power, just remember Johnny Carson's quote. **The truth is, we're the ones that have the total power.**

One of the great things about this quote and the underlying concept is that our market (or any other market) has very basic needs. Very rarely do people say, "You know what? I really need a CD-ROM with resale rights." What they say is, "I have a need for financial freedom," or "I have a need for significance or consistency," or "I have a need for a feeling of contentment." In many cases, **they know what will give them that feeling: having more friends or money. They've gotten to that point, it's up to us to meet them the rest of the way.** We are able to go to them and say, "If you want more money, I have a CD ROM with resale rights. Let me show you how that's going to fill your basic desire for financial freedom." Once we know that our customers have very basic wants, we can then say, "Okay, let's find a way to deliver a product or service that will give them the feelings they want." There's so much control there because there are thousands — maybe even tens or hundreds of thousands — of ways to give somebody those feelings of financial freedom, of consistency, or of contentment, that they're after. **So we're in complete control, and have this amazing power — if we focus on what their basic wants are — then we decide how we're going to deliver a product that meets what they want.**

For some people, Johnny Carson's statement that he's in complete control makes it seem like he was some sort of megalomaniac. But in fact, he was identifying the same consciousness of craft that a good actor or a good writer has. He was inside of this craft, and had accepted his professional responsibility. The audience wants to be emotionally moved. They want to be riveted to their seats. As the person who's responsible for the show, for the marketing push, for the work you're creating , you have to do it right — and you have to do it professionally rather than amateurishly.

Our customers are an audience, just like the people watching a talk show or a rock concert are an audience. They're out there and they want something. Our customers are tuning into our radio station to hear our program. **We**

have to give them what they want — and we have to keep giving it to them day after day, week after week, year after year. Once people decide they really like and want something, they very seldom tire of it; or at least, it might be years before they say, "You know, I'm going to do something else now." Fulfill what your audience desires. **Don't just find a need and fill it; find out what people's desires are and what they want, then give it to them, and you'll be successful.**

Here's a cautionary tale to go with that statement. Once you get into the business and understand it a little bit more, **you're going to come to the point where you want to deliver not what your customers want, but what you think they *should* want.** You say to yourself, "Okay, I know that they should want this, and that they should have it. I know it's going to meet their needs, so I'm going to create it, and I'm going to sell it to them." Then you go out there and you try to sell it to them — and they don't want it. That's a terrible problem to find yourself in because, obviously, you've lost some connection with the customer, even if you can't see how. You have to *always* connect with your customer.

It's very easy to say, "These people are a certain type of people, and the best thing for them would be this." At that point you're acting like a parent, telling little Johnny what would be best for them. Well, you know what? Johnny might not want what you're offering just because you think it's best for him — he may not even want it even if it really *is* best for him. Johnny wants what Johnny wants, and if he doesn't get it from you, he's going to go somewhere else to get it. **So even though you want to do what's best for your customers, you can only deliver that if you're giving them what they want.** Keep away from the trap of selling them what they *should* have and what you think they *should* want.

CHAPTER THIRTY

The money you spend on front-end marketing is an investment toward future profits.

Aggressive marketers are <u>not</u> making big profits on the first sale that they make to a customer. **The big profits all come in the reselling you do to the customers you bring in.** You must think of your business as a funnel. You have to increase the size of your funnel to make more money. **That just means that you're doing more front-end marketing to bring in new groups of customers, or prospects that you can turn into customers.**

There are just three ways to build a business: you have to either bring in more customers; make more sales to those customers more often; or get more money from each customer on every sale. That's it. Within those three categories, there are probably many, many different things you can try, and there are lots of different variables involved — but it's actually that simple. You can put that on a 3 x 5 index card, and have something that people write whole books about.

Bringing in more customers is one of basics things you have to do, but there are **two basic problems with that practice. The first is the fact that most business people**

care only about bringing in new customers. Once they get a customer, they leave them alone. They're constantly doing all kinds of front-end advertising to attract new customers, and they're not doing anything on the back end at all. In so doing, they're giving up a lot of their profits. **The second problem that I see is related to the first. Some people just stop doing front-end marketing altogether once they've established a customer base.** They depend on that customer base to make money — but the customer base evaporates after awhile, if only because people die and move away. I like to think of it as a pond. You have to replenish the pond; the water will evaporate over time so, unless you get some rain, there goes your pond; it's all going to dry up. You have to do things to keep filling that pond. Most marketers know if they can even break even on the front-end, they're incredible lucky. I don't think anyone is making any real money, anywhere, on the front end. There might be some people not losing too much or even breaking even, but even so, **all the profits are on the back end.**

To me, that's where the fun part of marketing, the real business, is. **You have a group of customers, and you have to try and do everything you can to squeeze as much money out of them as possible.** Now, I don't mean that in a bad way. You shouldn't cheat them, and you shouldn't lie to them. You shouldn't take advantage or manipulate them — but morally and ethically, you have to do everything you can to suck them dry! You have to take every last dollar of disposable income from them, as long as you're doing it morally and ethically, and you're being honest and sincere. Admittedly, despite that honesty and sincerity, there's a certain amount of ruthlessness here. There has to be. But where do you draw the line? You want to serve the customer and you're trying to help them; you're trying to give them value, but at the same time you're trying to suck every last penny of disposable income out of them. The great thing about it is that **you let the *customer* draw the line.** The customers are the ones who make the decisions. It's not like you're chasing them around, reaching into their wallet, and taking their money. You're not stealing it; you're going after them with offers and ways to try and get them to give you money, but it's up to them to respond — or even to pay attention to you. **It's their ultimate decision whether or not to give you any more money.** If they're tapped out or don't want any more, that's fine — they won't purchase from you. But if they have the money and the insatiable appetite that most customers do in this field, they're going to keep giving you more money, the more offers you send to them. **They're going to give it to somebody, so they may as well give it to you.**

Many people are insanely worried about competition, but I don't care about it; in fact, I pay little attention to competition. **What I want to do is own my customers.** When they become our customers, I care about them. Once they get into the fold, I want to do everything possible to get as much money out of them as I can, in legal, moral, and ethical ways. I'm not talking about ripping people off; I'm talking about getting them to give their disposable income to you instead of some another company in your market. That's something a lot of people forget, and it's part of the game. Each customer only has so much disposable income, and they're going to give that money to somebody. **You have to figure out how to make them give that money to you rather than someone else.** Make them realize you'll give them a huge amount of value, more than the other guys will — so much more that you leave them with a big, satisfied smile on their face.

You see, that sets up the next sale. It's not like you're just trying to turn them upside down and shake them until all their money falls out, and then you're going to scoop it up go run off somewhere. **If you're not keeping your customers happy, they ain't gonna come back — and it's when they come back that you make the real money.** That's part of the whole deal. That's why I don't want anybody to think I'm talking about cheating, or stealing, or abusing people, or taking advantage of them in any way — because if you do crap on them like that, they'll leave you. Unless they're a complete idiot, a person's only going to touch a hot stove one time. You don't want to be a hot stove. **You want customers to come back to you again and again — so you'd better make sure that you treat them right.**

While this is the best thing to do from an ethical standpoint, it's also interwoven with the economics of the situation. When you're getting your customer the first time, you have to divide the cost of acquiring that customer by the number of prospects you had to have some kind of interaction with. Whether you're paying for eZine ads or real magazine ads or renting lists, you're paying for the prospect universe. Only a few of the people who see your ad are going to buy. So let's just say that your cost per prospect is $3, and let's just say your cost per buyer is $20. In this case, it costs you $20 to make that front-end sale. That's just a theoretical statement; it could actually work out to anything. **However, making another sale will be easy if you're marketing to your email database; it costs zero, so all the money you get is profit.** Do it again and again, and it's all profit. You're dipping back into the pond I talked about earlier. Even if you're using Direct-Mail, like many of us still do in this Internet age, that's still only going to cost 80 cents to $1 per mailing. It's not going to cost the money you spend to get the customer the first time, so you're making more profit.

Plus, **there's a level of trust with a repeat customer that you don't get with a brand new front-end customer.** If you've done your job right as a marketer and delivered (or overdelivered) the quality you promised, your customers are going to feel they can trust you — and they know that if they're not happy with the product, they're going to get their money back. **If you deliver and satisfy your customer,**

you'll create another want in that customer. That's what you're really focusing on: delivery. If you really deliver something that they want, they're going to want to do business with you again. They're going to want to get more mailings from you, and they're going to want to hear about more products. If they have that desire to get a particular product from you or to hear from you again, boy, it's *so* much easier to make those sales. So while you want to be ruthless, to get all the money you can out of people, you really need to make the experience so entertaining, so enjoyable, so satisfying, and fulfilling that they can't wait to buy more stuff from you.

There are only one or two companies like that that I've bought from. And believe me — they can't create products fast enough to satisfy my needs! Any time they come out with something new, I'm right there with my credit card in hand, waiting to give the money to them. If you can build up that type of a relationship and build up that type of desire in your customers, you'll find it easy to make back-end sale after back-end sale. **But you have to be ready to serve those customers! They want to see what you've come up with for them.** When it comes to making money on the back end, some people have no clue as to what they're going to sell to their customers once they have them. They'll have one little widget, one book or report, one cassette tape or product or service — and after they sell that item, man, they're scratching their head. They can't figure out what in the world they're going to keep selling. Maybe you're feeling that way now.

One of the nicest products you can sell is the grand slam web promotion package, something like what my friends Jeff Gardner and Russ von Hoelscher recently created. It lasts three months, and then the customer can buy it again and again. When they make it available to their dealers, they can get four sales out of one website for every customer in one year. We're not the first people to come up with the idea; far from it. Kellogg's and General Mills, have made a ton of money because the people who eat Cheerios or Wheaties get to like them and buy them again and again.

I'd say you have to do two things to have an effective front end. **One, you need to have a product or service that can be used repeatedly — several times a year — or you need to have all kinds of back end offers that are similar to what you sold the first time.** They should be a natural, logical progression of products so that if they bought this product, then they should buy this product and the next one to make their lives better.

What I'm talking about here may sound, on one hand, so simple and so natural to us — but on the other hand, it can sound very complicated. Let me give you a true-life example. After his initial success, my colleague Ted Ciuba found himself in identically the position I was talking about earlier — what was he going to follow up that initial success *with*? He'd taken a three-day seminar and learned how to write a sales letter, so he wrote that sales letter and blasted out a manual. He was so happy because sales were brisk. Then he quite literally found that he had a mounting database and said to himself, "What am I going to do next? How can I harvest something? These people are interested." Here's how difficult it was. He thought a little bit and, since he knew his own field, it wasn't a real big challenge. Who had the best-selling comparable product? Ted identified that person and gave them a call. He said, "Hey, I'd like to make a deal. I have some customers to whom I'd like to mail out the sales letter you've already written. I thought it was a killer. We'll split the profits 50/50. Would that be okay?" The person said, "Yes!" So right there Ted had a back end product, another thing to sell the people who came in. **That's called a joint venture, and it's a very powerful strategy for building your back end.** It's the language that all of us in business understand when you say, "Would you like to make more money without doing anything?" Our ears all perk up and we say, "Sure!" It's not a very difficult situation to be in.

With the back end, you're offering customers products and services that are similar but different from products or services than they bought the first time. I recently read a very interesting article in *Forbes* magazine about Harley Davidson. The article talked about how the engineers at Harley Davidson spend an enormous amount of time thinking about how they could create brand-new motorcycles using all this brand-new technology they had, and *still* make them look just like the old Harley Davidsons — because they know that the customers want a certain type of thing. They have several different models of Harleys, so if you buy one Harley you're not necessarily satisfied. It doesn't stop there. You can get another model. The same is true with your business, too. You have to find similar but slightly different back-end items to offer to the people who bought from you the first time. There's a real art to it; it's not learned over night. **My best advice is to find successful companies in your market, get on their mailing list, and find out how they're using this principle.**

I've identified as a power metaphor something that a friend of mine talks about: the **"killer marketer."** He says, *"We smell blood every time one of our promotions works, and we only want more!"* This is short but sweet. I think that <u>what he's talking about is the feeling that we know very well when one of our promotions is working</u>. We suddenly feel energized. We're more able. We're more driven. We're excited. We're like the kid at the theme park at 4:00 in the afternoon. It ain't time to go home!

So, **success gets us more involved. It's an instinctive flow. It puts you on a new level; it's intuitive.** <u>Experience gives you power.</u> That's not exactly what I want to focus on here, but the truth is, with experience you instinctively know how to handle the many situations that confuse and frustrate those with less experience at being successful. Not only does it make you feel good when the money's coming in, since you're getting appreciation and you're contributing in a meaningful way, but it increases your expertise and your ability. You feel more competent; you're energized; you can run faster, go faster, shoot longer. I think it's like a hunt: you're on the prowl for more sales and profits. **You have to have fun with it.** I never, ever get tired of this business because there are so many new things to do. You can learn so many things. No matter how much you learn, there's more to learn. I forget some of the techniques that I used 10 years ago that worked, and then all of a sudden Ted Ciuba or Jeff Gardner or Russ von Hoelscher will say something, and I'll think, "Wow, that worked great for me in 1994 — I have to do it again."

The learning never stops. I have a friend who hunts deer with a bow. I have no interest in that whatsoever, but given the way he describes it and the enthusiasm he has for the topic, I can't help but be interested when I listen to him talk about how he's elevated it to an art form, and about the years he's spent perfecting his ability to go out with a single bow and some arrows on his back, and come back with a deer. (I thought this was totally barbaric until I found out that there are too many deer out there, and that a lot of people are getting killed because they're overpopulated.) Anyway, his game is becoming the very, very best hunter that he can possibly be. A lot of his friends are also hunters, but they're not perfecting their skills like he is. They'll go out and spend a whole day and won't get anything whereas he will because he's perfected his skills as a hunter.

I think that's the kind of thing that all of us, as marketers, have to do. **The more we do that, the better we get; the better we get, the more money we make; and the more money we make, the more we want to get better!** Then you see these younger guys coming into the market and all of a sudden they're doing really well, and it makes you envious, but in a good way. Now you want to say, "Hey, if they can do it, I can, too!"

Again, that's part of the game: not only competing with yourself, but competing with others. **Business is a *sport*, which means it's not a game of chance.** Technique, choices, preparation, timing, adopting and embracing new philosophies all make a really big difference in your game and consequent enjoyment. Guess what? We score with dollars, which happens to be my favorite game! In fact, it's the greatest game of all!

Let me re-emphasize one thing: **the better you get, the better you *want* to get.** In the beginning, it's all just about the money you can make; that's all that people want. That's all *I* wanted in the beginning — a bunch of money. I didn't care about any of this other stuff. I didn't want to learn marketing, or how to write copy. After a while, though, the money becomes less of an issue.

My mentor Russ von Hoelscher told me that when he started out, what he wanted was a nice house and a Cadillac, and to take some nice vacations. Then he got a Cadillac and a nice house by a lake in Minnesota, and took trips to lots of places, including England and France — and then he said to myself, "Is that all there is?" Suddenly, the Caddy wasn't good enough any more. The house didn't necessarily make him happy, even though it could be a sanctuary. He also discovered he'd rather be in America than in Europe. That's the point where you say to yourself, *"I have to do this for some reason other than the money and the toys."* I think that's where the game part comes in. **It's a *mental* game.** It's a game where you're writing things and getting people to respond to them, and then you're fulfilling their needs while you're making money. It's fun. It's energizing. It's exciting. It's something where you can just say, "This is a meaningful life. It's all good." **Then what becomes important is growing as a marketer, trying to learn more, trying to develop your skills.**

Before I talked about business as a sport, and that's a powerful analogy, because it takes a lot of practice to be great at any sport. You need training and coaches; you need to work with people. If it weren't for Russ von Hoelscher working with us back in 1989 and helping to guide us along the road, we would never have made it. I think that people who believe they can get to their ultimate goals without going through all those steps, in business or whatever, are kidding themselves. **The more time you put into it, the more time you focus on it, the more time you really hone your skills, the better you'll be.**

Take Tiger Woods, for example, who was out playing golf when he was three years old. He had some natural ability, and through lots of practice and steady work every day in his craft, he's still at the top of his game as of this writing. Just like golf, **making money is all about learning and honing your craft** — in this case, writing and studying every day. **The more you do it the better you get.** If you want to make it in the NBA or NFL or Major League baseball, you're not going to get there by just piddling around and dilly-dallying. You're going to get there by playing the game for hours at a time, by studying every day, and by watching and studying other people who are already doing what you want to do and who are where you want to be. That's how you become great.

There's a quote that says, *"The joy is in the pursuit."* Everybody's always saying, "Well, if I just had this, or if I just had that... " **But it's not the end result, necessarily, that makes you happy; it's the chase.** That's where the fun is. That's where the thrill is. That's where the joy is. Yes, the money is wonderful, and it's a good way to keep score — but it's not really important in the long run. I promise you, if somebody had a gun to the head of the person you love the most in this world and they said, "Give me all your money or I'm squeezing this trigger," you'd say, "Here, take it all. I'll go get some more."

So, money is fun. It's counters in a game. We all start out just wanting money, but then we find there are things you have to do to get it, and the more we can fall in love with those things — well, **that's where the real joy comes in.** After you get the house and the car and your bills are paid, what else is it good for?

A rich attorney once told Russ von Hoelscher about a rich client of his. The lawyer said, "I like rich clients who are in danger of going to jail." This particular client was a rich man and was in trouble for tax evasion in Minneapolis. The lawyer said, "You know what he'll pay me to stay out of jail? Every damn cent he has!"

If you were freezing to death in some little cabin that had no electricity or no heat, and all you had was $1 million stacked up in twenty dollar bills, you know what? You'd burn that money all night just to stay alive. Let me repeat this: **it's not really the money that matters — it's this other stuff.** Yes, it does mean you have to dedicate your life, to a certain degree, to really becoming the best you can be when it comes to marketing — but it's rewarding in many ways beyond the money, too.

CHAPTER THIRTY-ONE

If you confuse them, you might sell them.

Sometimes you must keep things simple, and sometimes you must confuse them. Confusion can be your biggest selling tool. **The more confused people are, the more complicated something seems to be, the easier it is for them to give you huge sums of money to do everything for them.**

Let me tell you a story to illustrate this. There's a copywriter who created a course on writing ad copy. It's an incredible course, but it's huge. He goes into absurd detail on everything: writing the guarantee, writing the headline, the text, everything. It's just a massive, monster course. There are videotapes and audiotapes included with it. The entire course is just about how to write sales copy. Believe me, if you even get through the course, by that time do you don't even *want* to write a sales letter. By the time you're done you say, "Oh my goodness, there are so many things that go into writing a sales letter that I don't want to do it myself! I want to hire the person who wrote this guide!" *That's what why he wrote it.* He created this package, certainly, with the intention of making some money by teaching people how to write ad copy, but he made it so intense and with so much detail because he knew he would get a lot of copywriting jobs from people who purchased it and said, "Look, I don't want to mess with this. I don't have the time. I just want to give you $5,000 or $10,000 to do it for me." **He got a lot of business by creating this product that confused people so much, and made them**

realize that writing copy can be difficult, that they wanted to give him money to do it for them. I don't know if that's good or if it's great, but the fact is, you can confuse people as much as you need to in order to make them give you money.

I took a communications class one time where we were told to write out instructions on how to create a peanut butter and jelly sandwich. That's pretty simple. Anybody can do that. But the teacher said, "It's not as simple as you think. Let's say someone came from a different planet, and they'd never heard of peanut butter. They had never heard of jelly. They had never heard of a sandwich or bread. They don't know how to use utensils. They don't know how to take the tops off of jars or canisters. *Now* write the instructions." People literally had 20, 30, 50, and 100 pages worth of instructions saying things like, "Now you hold the bread horizontally in the palm of your hand with your fingers outstretched." We're talking *detailed*. If you want to really use the power of confusion by showing your clients that a certain process is so complicated that they don't want to do it themselves, that's certainly one way to go. You may decide you don't want to use that method, but it's available, and it's a very effective method indeed. **You see, confusion equals pain.** When people are confused, they're in a lot of pain. **So, what you want to do is help confuse them, and then offer your product or service as the solution.**

Just think about H & R Block, the tax service. H & R Block is built on confusion. The tax laws are so complex and baffling that you really have to be a rocket scientist to understand them. They're thousands of pages long. People are so confused by them that they say, "Look, I could certainly get the manual and read all this stuff and figure it out myself. But hey, I can go down to H & R. Block and have them do it for me. I'm more than happy to give up this pile of money than to try and figure it out myself."

All of us have to sell solutions, and **sometimes the best way to sell those solutions is to take the problem and make it worse.** Some of us are in business to help people get into their own business. They're already frustrated. They're already confused. We just help to make them a little bit more so. **We help them feel that pain, and then offer our products or services — solutions to that pain.** Even if there isn't an immediate problem, we want to amp it up and make it seem real and emotional and connected, so they feel motivated to act now. You offer the ointment, which is what they buy because we say, "We're here to help you. We're going to get you started, and we're going to do a lot of the work for you." That's what people want since, at first, everything seems so overwhelming. **They just want some help.**

In most cases, people are already in pain. Fear is a basic part of all people's lives. They're confused, and they're searching. If they weren't, in most markets they wouldn't even be doing business with you. They never would have answered any of your ads or sent for any of your materials. They're already in pain. They're already confused. **Often they're already frustrated, and we just play into that more and more, and then offer our own products or services as the solution.**

CHAPTER THIRTY-TWO

Our prospective buyers and customers don't give a damn about us, our companies, or our products and services.

All your prospects and customers care about is themselves. But if we qualify our prospects, we also know that they *do* care about owning the benefits of what we offer. This is our power over them. **We must build so much value into our offers that it breaks down their resistance to buy.**

Too often, we fool ourselves into thinking our customers care about us. Maybe they do in some cases, but that's usually not the case. **They like us for what we can do for them,** not necessarily because they're our buddies. We may get into the mindset that they care about our company and our success when they really don't. The one thing they do care about, and they absolutely care about it an awful lot, **is themselves.** They want your offer to answer one important question, and that's WIIFM — **What's In It For Me? That's the most important thing on their minds when they see your offer,** whether it's a mail offer or an Internet offer. The reason they're there at that moment is to find out what your product is, or what it can do for them. We are absolutely (and I'm sure you're aware of this) a very selfish society. We usually care only about what a specific offer will do for us. Unfortunately, that's also why charitable contributions aren't what they should be, and why we'll more quickly throw away a letter that asks us to donate money than one that asks us to give up money to get a benefit in return.

So when it comes to creating your offer, you have to remember this one simple rule: **the audience doesn't care about you and who you are.** Another important point to remember is that they really don't even care about your specific product or service. I know that a lot of times we tend to fall in love with our products and services as marketers, but that's the wrong way to go. **Our customers don't care about our products and services** *themselves.* **All they want is what the product or service you can do for them.** They want the benefit that you're offering.

If you're in the health industry and have a magic pill, they really don't care about the actual pill that you're offering them; they care how it works for them or makes them feel. They're buying the glamour of weight loss if it's a weight loss pill. If it's a vitamin, they care about the benefit that taking that pill every day is going to give them. A customer buying a car doesn't see that you're really trying to sell them a two-ton pile of metal. They buy the sexiness of being in a brand new convertible. They're not seeing the product; **they're seeing the benefit that they're going to receive from the product.**

Along those same lines, we have to create so much value in our offers that our customers can't help but open their wallets and give us their money. **The one important thing that each promotion you create has to do is build tremendous value.** If you're selling a tape and a book, or a book and a couple of tapes, don't just tell people that. Instead of just presenting it as a cut-and-dried product that will increase your sales and profits. Make it more glamorous than it really is by using the benefit copy to talk about what the offer will do for them. *That's all they really care about.*

We call this the "piling on" technique. You make an offer, you describe the featured product, and you add so much value to it in bonuses, gifts, and additional features that it becomes so valuable they almost can't say no. You pile on additional benefit after additional benefit, bonus after bonus, and first thing you know it's so big that if the prospect had any interest in the product in the beginning, by the end it's become a no-brainer for them to decide to go ahead and buy it. In many cases we use a formula where we gave more in bonuses than the value of the product we are selling. So, if we were selling a $195 product, we would offer $200 or $250 in bonuses. If the customer had any inclination at all to make the purchase, then we just kind of pushed them over.

We have a $3,000 promotion out there right now that has a true value of $30,247.50, which we make sure we point out to our prospects. **The golden key here is that people have to actually *believe* it.** You have to go on and on, and try and prove it, and then you have to have a really great reason they should buy — or they won't. They don't care about your overhead or employees or your mortgage payment or your kids; they want benefits for themselves. The more you can give them a reason to buy it the better because you know they're skeptical. People are so damn skeptical it's not even funny. They have every right to be, because there are a lot of sharp marketers out there trying to get their money. You have to come up with a powerful reason for why you're selling something, and you have to show them so it's not all just hype. **Once they start thinking you're hyping it up too much, you've lost their trust. Once you've lost their trust, you've lost their money.**

That's an edge that we all have to walk as marketers. **We'll never satisfy everybody.** It gets back to what I mentioned in an earlier section: don't worry about who you offend, just count the sales. You have to do it that way. I have people who've come up to me and said, "What? You're putting a value of $97 on that audio CD? Everybody knows you can get an audio CD for $9.97." Then someone else will come up and say, "Wow, man, you guys are really hot. You shouldn't be selling that CD for anything less than three times what you're charging!" **So with price, we'll never get it right exactly. It's not the cassette that brings the value: it's always the benefit.**

We could even take this concept one step further. In one of the sales letters that Ted Ciuba has out there right now, he's selling a product for $497. The letter goes to people who already have some activity in Internet Marketing and traditional Direct-Response Marketing, but who probably don't have exactly what they want as far as revenues go. Ted starts right off with, "Hey, you've had a taste, and now you long for the wealth and independence that your own successful marketing can bring you." In other words, it's not, "We're going to sell you another super program," it's the wealth and independence that's important. Here's what you want: more quality time with your family, a new car, a bigger, finer house, privileged school for the kids, expensive clothes, fine dining, travel, security for your future years, and the respect and prestige that comes with success. *It all comes back to benefits.* People don't buy material, **they buy benefits. They want what it'll do for them.** When we create a vast picture of all the benefits, real and perceived, that's when they spend their money.

I think some of the greatest lessons out there right now are in Direct-Response television. Earlier, I was talking about **"piling on."** Remember the Ginsu knives that were big back in the '80s or the early '90s? You get these five knives, and they show you all five and then say, "But wait, there's more! You'll also get this knife and this knife. But wait, there's still more!" Recently they've come up with all kinds of innovative ways to sell plastic. They have this new little commercial out there right now that's for moving men. I bought the product because it shows these little, bitty ladies who are barely 100 pounds, who look like they're anorexics, moving huge furniture all around the house effortlessly. Then they show these big 300-pound monster guys who are struggling and straining to lift the furniture — but if you put this little piece of plastic under the furniture, a little lady can practically push it with one finger. Then they make the offer where they give you so many of these piece of plastic for $19.95 — and then they say, "But wait, if you order now you'll also get..." and by the time the commercial's over it looks like you're going to get so much crap for $19.95 that you just can't stand it! So when they ask for $19.95, you say, "Well, it might be worth it." That's what I said when I watched it. Then they added another set, and five more miniature ones, and then they added something else, so suddenly it becomes, "Hey, that's a good deal!" Then you get the box and realize you just bought $2 worth of plastic!

They're getting really creative on these infomercials. One of the most successful infomercials recently has been for the Turbo Cooker. It's a stovetop cooker that cooks and bakes and air fries and does a lot of things. My friend Russ von Hoelscher bought one, and he likes it; he uses it quite often. They've sold something like a million of them for $79.95 — so that's $80 million. Another company went into production real quick to go into competition with the Turbo Cooker, and they called theirs the Quick Cooker. They show pretty much the same infomercial with different people, but then they say, "But wait — if you order in the next 30 minutes we'll give you two Quick Cookers!" **The "buy one and get one free" deal is probably the oldest sales inducement in the world... And it still works like magic!**

One thing more about building up the bonuses: you still have to sell those as well. You shouldn't just list them. Sometimes you have to because of space requirements, but if you have an option, you need to sell the value of those as well.

If you're going to add a tape and assign a value of $39 or $49 or $75, you need to tell them why it's worth that much money; otherwise you run the risk of looking like you're just inflating prices. That destroys credibility, so you need to make it real. You tell the story and explain it all. You make them *want* it. A bonus has no value if the customers don't want it. Sometimes people really shortchange that. They just list the items you're also going to get without trying to sell those, too — and remember, **if you do things right, your customers may want the free bonuses more than they want anything else.**

But be careful: don't go through your warehouse and pick out the stuff that didn't sell and offer it as free bonuses or free gifts. Avoid your natural thought, which is, "If I'm going to give stuff away, I'm going to give away the stuff that didn't sell." That's just the opposite of what you should do. If something didn't sell, that means it has no power — so why add it as bonus? It's not something people wanted, and it's just more to ship. **Find something people are dying for and can't get any other way, and make that your free bonus.** That's why some people subscribe to *Sports Illustrated* magazine — just to get that swimsuit edition.

Russ von Hoelscher told us a few years ago that there was a time when he honestly felt that you should limit the amount of bonuses that you give because you didn't want to make your offers too unbelievable — and now he's changed your mind about that. He says it's because was **there was a time when people had more common sense!** If you made things sound too good back then, you were afraid of a backlash of skepticism. But advertising has gone in such a crazy direction in the past 20 or 30 years that you can't give more benefits without getting more sales. Nowadays you can sell something that you claim is worth $10,000 for $99, even if it's not, because people want instant gratification and they want more, more, more. **It seems that can't make the offer**

too strong without getting more business.

Even if people think, "Oh, there's no way it's worth that!" they'll still get the idea that, *"But maybe it's worth a hell of a lot more than they're asking."* And if you're selling something for $99 and you tell them it's worth $10,000, a rational human being is going to say "Bull! But maybe for $99 I'll get a $1,000 worth of value, and that's a good deal."

In one of our most successful seminars, we gave people 100 websites free just for coming, and we showed them that each of those websites had a value of X amount of money. The whole pitch was that everything they got for coming to this $5,000 seminar was worth $168,000. When we first created that offer, I thought, "Man, we're really going over the top on this one." I really thought we were pushing it too hard, but I was in a mindframe, at the time, where I wanted to see how far I *could* push it. Sure enough, we had one seminar and we sold out. We had to create a second seminar for all the people who couldn't get into the first one. I think that a lot of people absolutely, positively didn't believe in any way, shape or form that they were really getting $168,000 worth of value, but they did believe that what they got was worth a hell of a lot more than that $5,000. I know there's probably such a thing as taking it too far — maybe I spend too much time worrying about that — **but I do know that of you offer something for $5,000, you must deliver at least $5,000 in value.**

We even made arguments about that in our letter. We showed them how other people were charging more than $5,000 for a seminar that didn't give you anything. You just came and sat for three days and took notes. Then you went bye-bye and were $5,000 poorer and you got nothing. Of course, they didn't know they were going to spend $6,000 for the hernia operation to carry home all the stuff that we were going to give them!

We've always given great values at these seminars. **They may be $5,000 seminars, but very few if any people leave those seminars without feeling very good about their purchase.** Russ von Hoelscher was recently telling me about a woman came up to him at that seminar and said, "Two weeks ago I was in Hawaii with a popular marketer, and I spent $15,000 for four or five days just to hear speakers tell me how to make money and to try and build me up with motivation and then give me a little moneymaking information. I came to this seminar for $5,000. I got as much good information here as I did on the $15,000 seminar, but I took home five boxes of materials that can put me in business for myself. So it's a hundred times better deal for me!"

Adam Smith, the nation's first economist, once said, "You can't put two capitalists in a room together for more than 30 minutes before they start talking about how to cheat the public out of their money." I don't necessarily agree with that. The bottom line is, I don't care how ruthless a marketer you are — **if you're not giving your customers value, then you're not going to get the real fortune that can be made, which is in the back end.** Hey, you can screw somebody once and maybe get away with it, but you just can't keep on screwing people over and over and expect that they're going to automatically come back again. Like they say, you can shear a sheep several times a year — but you can only skin them once! I call it Ruthless Marketing, but nowhere am I advocating cheating. **I'm really advocating being educated and intelligent, strategic and calculating in getting the most money from your market.**

I also recommend that you do all you can to get the market excited about what you have to offer so you can sell them, and also to help them see the benefits that are in what's being offered. So often the benefits aren't obvious to everyone. **If you can help them see those benefits and also get them excited about them, then that's not really hype.**

You may label it as such because of the enthusiasm you express, but really, it's doing the customer a service. If the benefit's there for him and you can help him see those benefits, that's good selling.

The worst scoundrels I've seen in this business are those people who pretend to be altruistic. They say they're going to do all these great things for you, and there's nothing in it for them. Well, that's pure B.S. **because an honorable marketer is going to do everything he can for his customer — but he also expects to make some money in the process.** So if anyone tells you they're going to do everything for you and there's nothing in it for themselves, you'd better run like hell, because they're out to fleece you.

You see? **It's all about the benefits your product can offer your customers, not how much they like you and care about you making a profit.** People don't buy from us just because they think we're nice people. On the other hand, **I *do* believe they'll often buy from us when they feel they're a lot like us.** So, I think it's important to put a personality on your marketing and put a face on your company, and to use sales letters to tell a story about yourself — but not to aggrandize yourself. In fact, **it's good to use some humility.** People often buy from people they perceive to be a lot like them.

When we first got started in the business in the 1980s, there were still a lot of these full-page get-rich-quick ads. You'd get the opportunity magazines and in some there's be as many as 40-50 full-page ads. A lot of those ads showed people standing in front of limousines, in front of big houses, wearing tuxedoes and fancy dress clothing. When we first hired Russ von Hoelscher to help us with our marketing, we said to him, "Hey Russ, we're thinking about going out and renting a limousine and having our picture taken in front of some fancy house in Wichita." He said, "Guys, that's the stupidest thing I've ever heard! If you do that you're going to ruin everything!" He spent a lot of time teaching us about the principle of **putting a real face on the business.** He told us, "You guys are just a couple of little country bumpkins out here in Goessel, Kansas — the middle of nowhere. You want to try to tell people, *"Hey, here we are, just a couple of country bumpkins out here in the middle of nowhere, and if we can make money, you can make money! If a couple of dumb people like us can get rich, you can get rich."* Because people in Kansas are perceived as being honest and trustworthy and down-home folks — good people — that's exactly what Russ wanted Eileen and I to be perceived as.

I was talking to a customer in Dallas, Texas, recently — one of those few who's aggressively trying to go out there and get something done. I was saying, "Bill, you need a story. You need to *tell* people your story." He said the same thing to me that I said to Russ back in 1989: "I really don't have a story." I said, "Bull, man, you *do* have a story. You've sent away for all these get-rich quick programs for the last 10 years, and you've been ripped off countless times, and now you have something solid you want to offer them. Talk about your pain, your struggle. **Let people identify because they've gone through the same things that you have." There's a term for this: affinity marketing and it will make you <u>massive</u> sums of money! So start using it!**

CHAPTER THIRTY-THREE

Blur the lines between your work and play.

When I was starting out, I bought into the whole idea that if I just had money, everything was going to be okay in my life. I had some real personal problems when I was younger, and I was all messed up. I bought into this whole notion that if I just had enough money, if I just had a nice house and a nice car, everything would be fine. But one of the most depressing times I've been through in my life was after we got started and we had a little success. All of a sudden the money was pouring in, and I realized that I didn't feel any different. I went through about six months of depression because I expected something that just wasn't there. Then, Russ von Hoelscher helped set me straight and snap me out of my depression. He had some very good advice for me at the time I needed it the most.

Basically, **Russ just showed me that in a business like this, the money's just a nice little by-product, and that's all it is.** I try to teach this to people who are on the way up. **The real joy in this business is all of the things you do to _get_ the money.** I think Direct-Response Marketing, whatever the medium you use, is the greatest game on Earth. It's just a hell of a lot of fun. I'd like people to experience this for themselves. When you're in the game, you're trying new ideas all the time; you're coming up with all these creative ideas and, depending on the media you're using when you come up with the idea, you can end up raking in the dough very quickly.

Here's an example. One recent Christmas Eve, we were planning to take off work at noon. Right before we took off that day, my Vice President Randy Hamilton, came up to me and said, "Hey, I think you should look at the figures from this small test we did." I'd forgotten all about this test. Right after he gave me those figures I got all excited and started working on a sales letter. I worked on it all that day and Christmas day, while Eileen and I sat and watched reruns of the Sopranos. It wasn't long afterward that we rolled out the letter, and the money started rolling in. Because Direct-Mail is such a fast medium, if you get good at it and have good suppliers, the length of time from the birth of an idea to the time you actually start getting the first money can be very short. In the meantime, you're on the edge with anticipation. You come up with a good idea, throw yourself into it, and get it done relatively quickly. Some sales letters can be done in a few days. I'm sure some people can even do them in a few hours, although I will never be one of those people.

There's this amazing level of anticipation as you're waiting for the orders to come in because now you just can't wait to see how it's going to work. You wake up in the morning, and when the first order comes in, you're just so damn excited; and then when you actually hit break-even day, from then on it's profit. After that it gets so thrilling to go in everyday to find out, how many orders did we get? How many sales are we getting on this or that? **It's the game here that I want to really try to impress this upon people. It's not the goal or the money, so much.** I like what Jim Rhone says. He says, *"It's not the goal, it's the person you become as you reach for that goal."* As you challenge yourself to become a better marketer, you're going to have to develop some real skills here.

There's a ton of stuff to learn, though I don't mean that in

---

a bad way. I think it's exciting as hell, because no matter how much you learn, **you can always learn more. The big reward is the accomplishment you get.** It's the feeling of achievement. It's the satisfaction that you get from developing your powers. The fun is in doing all the things that you have to do to make the money. **It's the chase that's important.** Once you get something, all of a sudden if that's all it is, just getting it, then the fun goes out of it. You have to keep coming up with new things to chase after. **You have to stay hungry.** You're always on the pursuit —just like a high school boy is always out there chasing girls!

It's a game, then, and the **money is just one of the ways you keep score. For some people it's more important than others.** I like the feedback. I like the excitement , the feeling of accomplishment in seeing how well you've performed. I think the reason so many people enjoy watching sports on TV is because it's a substitute for game-playing in their own lives. They have jobs where they don't have a chance to play and tryout and win; they just do what they're told, and that's not seen as a win. So they have a favorite team, and they love to sit in front of the television sets and get excited because when their team wins, they win! It's exciting for them!

Well, direct marketing allows for the same thing. Every project you put out there has a chance to be a real winner for you. **You get to compete against yourself or other people, and the scorekeeping is very real.** It's the number of sales; it's the number of dollars. It makes a real difference. It's very much an exciting game. Dollars are more or less objective; in other words, if I write a poem and bring it to you and you tell me, "Oh, this is nice. This is really good," you could be lying through your teeth, just trying to make me feel good. But when we move into the marketing arena, **the value of what you've written lies in whether that sales letter makes you give me your money.** You can tell me, "Hey, that's neat, that's great!" But if you give me your money, I've won. Being a game, of course, **you're not always going to win.** Anybody with experience knows that results are always variable.

Gary Halbert once said that when he was writing books and manuals, he'd share them with this clique of friends. He had three or four buddies he'd meet with, and they'd have a few beers and pizza or whatever while he'd share his sales copy with them. When the guys said, "Hey, that's great, Gary. That sounds really good! Great idea!" That didn't mean crap. But when they would ask him, "Hey, when is that going to be out? Will you give me a copy, or can I buy one?" That's when he knew he had a winner. So take that to heart. When you share things with family or friends and they tell you they like your idea, that doesn't mean anything. **But, when they say, "I want that as soon as it's available," then you know you have something special.**

As my friend and colleague Don Bice once pointed out, it's hard to get over the amazement of having someone send you hundreds of dollars without them ever meeting you, just because you've written a letter and sent it to them. I've never gotten over the amazement of that. **The money is the feedback. It tells me how good of job you did, and that's very exciting.** It's a huge victory.

One of the famous Direct-Response guys who teaches other people how to write copy uses the analogy of an alchemist. He teaches people how to become an alchemist. At one point, I didn't even know what that word meant. I looked it up in the dictionary and I found that back in the 14th or 15th century, all of the kings and queens spent a considerable sum of their money on guys who were trying to turn base metals like lead into gold. I think it's a very useful analogy because you take words and you put them on paper or a computer screen, or you verbalize them on an audio CD.

This is such an exciting way to make a living! **I hope you'll get excited from reading this, and that it'll push you over the edge into making the commitment to marketing.** Once you do get into it, it tends to exert this pull on you. For some of us, it consumes your life. Pretty soon it takes over because there are so many interesting aspects of marketing that encompasses all areas. You start seeing things you've never seen before. You start thinking about things you've never thought about. You start coming up with better and better ideas. It's just a thrilling game!

CHAPTER THIRTY-FOUR

Delegate more!

Many people try to do everything themselves, and they never achieve major success. This is a big issue for a lot of us, particularly small business entrepreneurs and those just getting started. I'm guilty of this myself. **We want to do everything ourselves.** Sometimes it's because we want to stretch, and sometimes it's just because we don't want to spend the money. But we find all sorts of logical reasons for this behavior.

Number one, you can save money by doing it yourself. Number two, it's just easier to do it yourself than to explain to someone else how to do it because they'll never do it right. But those two excuses can hamper your success. If you're in business, you've probably used these arguments — and they're working against you. You may have boundless energy and think you have time to spare, but there are better uses for that time. **What's at the root of those excuses for doing it all yourself? It's really fear and control.**

Let's talk about control first. **Most of us are in business for ourselves because we want to control things.** We want control over our working hours. We want to control over where we work, when we work, how we work, which ideas are used. Most of all, we want control over our future. We feel more comfortable when we're controlling where we're headed, and maybe more secure. Let's face it: we don't really go into business to work less hours and to have more time off.

That's just a myth. If you've ever been in business for yourself, you know that. **We go into business to take control of our lives and we hesitate to give up that control to others for any reason.** Small business owners are usually terrible at delegating work.

The other side of our reluctance is the fact that **we're secretly afraid someone else won't do the job to our satisfaction.** We want it done exactly the way we want it done. That's more control. Even if it's in an arena we don't excel at, we're still more comfortable doing it ourselves. For example, maybe you're a good copy writer, but your ads and sales letters are lackluster; in most cases, you'll still struggle with those tasks rather than assign them to a professional or to someone else in your company. Maybe you aren't good at accounting. I'm guilty of that, but I still keep my own books. You might say, "Well, we're a small company, and I don't have all the employees to delegate to." Sure, you may not have someone working on your staff to do it, but there are outside sources you can use.

That's why this principle says that when we do all this ourselves, we're really a little lazy. **It means that we're not willing to pay someone else to do the job for us — and when we don't, a number of bad things can happen because we spend our time not doing things we're not really good at.** When you pay someone else to do it, it leaves you free time to concentrate on those aspects of the business that you do better than anyone you could hire because there are some things that you do that you do better than anyone else you could hire. Those are the things you're going to focus on.

I know that in my own business, I've made every mistake possible. That's my foolishness, and I think that there are a lot of people who share my foolishness. **In my case, my time is much better spent creating new product and sales copy**

than it is in taking care of operational items. Just imagine how much more profitable it would have been for my company if I took the hours I spend handling things other people can do better and instead created new products, new sales letters, or ads — because those are the things that I do well. Now, if I'd be a little more lazy and get other people to do some of that work for me, it would increase my success — and the same would be true for you. I mentioned earlier that **no one gets rich by themselves. The beginning entrepreneur tends to forget that;** they think they have to do it all, and that's just not the case.

So, how do you get over this habit of doing it all yourself and not asking for help? Well, my buddy Jeff Gardner has a really good way — remember, he simply calculated how much his time was worth per hour, and posted it on the wall. It turned out to be a real big figure. Now when something comes up that needs to be done, he looks up at that rate on the wall and says, "Do I really want to pay that for the job?" That makes it pretty easy to decide no, he can find someone else to do that while he does what he's better at. That's a very good, imaginative solution, and it keeps him focused because it keeps him from spending hundreds of dollars an hour sticking stamps on an envelope. He spends his time creating new products, new offers, and writing sales letters — those things he'd be hard-pressed to find someone else who could do as well as he does.

There are consultants who can help you with various aspects of your marketing. People like Russ von Hoelscher have been very helpful to us over the years; we've also gotten help from Don Bice, Ted Ciuba, Jeff Gardner, and of course Chris Lakey. **But you should never delegate your marketing.** I think it's that comfort zone thing, where you end up spending the majority of your time doing easier things. Let's face it. Some of this is tough. Everybody knows it in their hearts. You read these books, you hear our ideas, and now you have to start asking yourself harder questions. It's easier to do a bunch of crap that other people can do than to do the really tough stuff that only *you* can do.

I think that's another aspect of Ruthless Marketing: Being ruthless on yourself and asking yourself, **"Is this the best use of my time at this moment?"** Those of us in executive positions know that this is a trap that we'll fall into a lot of times, too. It's easier for us just to do something rather than spend the time it takes to teach someone to do it right, and then to let them handle it forever after. **We overlook the fact that once we've have taught them, then they can do it for us satisfactorily in the future.**

Now we're living in a day and age that I think is the most exciting period to be alive because you have all kinds of options available to you. We have Federal Express and computer modems. We have temporary services now, so you don't even have to go out and hire full-time employees. If things get busy, you just hire a bunch of temps — and then you get rid of them when things slow down a little bit. You're not making any commitment whatsoever to a temp. Thanks to the Internet, you can actually hire people online. For example, our graphic artist was recently learning how to do websites. She was getting to the point where she could eventually probably do one of them per day. Then we found out about this service on the Internet that people all over the world are hooked up to, and now we have people all over the world designing websites for us. Some days Chris Lakey, who works with me, gets as many as four or five of these websites done. One of our website guys is in Calcutta, India. It's just amazing to me that there's this company in Calcutta, India, with four guys who work 24-hour shifts. Two of them work twelve hours, and then the other two come in and work the other twelve hours, and they're doing business with people all over the world. **I think it's so exciting that you have these resources available to the average person today**

that were never available before. There's expertise available at very reasonable prices all over the Internet, and you never have to see the people face-to-face to get the work done. You never even have to talk to them on the telephone.

You know, when you pay a small amount of money to somebody in Calcutta, what we think of as a pittance they may consider a very good livelihood because the standard of living there is so much lower. **So, this is a way to help third-world people while we get something done at a very reasonable rate.** It's amazing because it costs as little as $25 for a website, though some of them go up to $100 or more. Jeff Gardner has people all over the world doing a variety of things for him besides just website design. They're doing ghostwriting, editing, and all kinds of other projects. The world has shrunk, and that gives the average person, like you and me, more power than they ever had before.

Think about that as you set out to use all of the little-known marketing strategies in this book!

www.ingramcontent.com/pod-product-compliance
Lightning Source LLC
Chambersburg PA
CBHW020202200326
41521CB00005BA/220